ABU ʿALI AL ....

THE JUDGMENTS OF NATIVITIES

TRANSLATED FROM THE LATIN VERSION
OF JOHN OF SEVILLE

BY

JAMES H. HOLDEN, M.A.

First Printing 1988
ISBN Number: 0-86690-339-9
Library of Congress Catalog Card Number: 88-70460

Cover Design: Betsy Estep

Published by:
American Federation of Astrologers, Inc.
P.O. Box 22040, 6535 South Rural Road
Tempe, Arizona 85282

Printed in the United States of America

TO

THE MEMORY OF

MARY ELLEN JONES

Who taught me
to read.

TABLE OF CONTENTS

TABLE OF CONTENTS

TABLE OF CONTENTS

INTRODUCTION

Abu 'Ali al-Khayyat.

Abu 'Ali al-Khayyat (c.770-c.835) was an Arabian astrologer, who flourished in the early years of the 9th century. Al-Nadim, the 10th century author of the celebrated *Fihrist* or Catalogue of Arabic literature, has this to say about him:

> He was Abu 'Ali Yahya ibn Ghalib, also called Isma'il ibn Muhammad, a pupil of Ma Sha Allah and one of the most excellent of the astrologers. Among his books there were:
>
> The Introduction; Questions; The Meaning; Governments (Dynasties); Nativities; Revolution of the Years of Nativities; The Prism, which he wrote for Yahya ibn Khalid; The Rod of Gold; Revolution of the Years of the World; Al-Nukat.[1]

Of the ten books listed by al-Nadim, only two (Questions and Nativities) are known to survive in Arabic. His book on Nativities was translated into Latin by Plato of Tivoli in 1136 and again by John of Seville in 1153. It is the second of these translations that was edited and published at Nürnberg, Germany, by Joachim Heller in 1546 and reprinted in 1549.[2] So far as I am aware, Abu 'Ali's book has not previously been translated into any modern language. However, an astrologer using the pseudonym "Senex" wrote an article "Gleanings from the old Astrologers" that appeared in the English periodical *Modern Astrology* (September 1930 and subsequent issues) in which he gave the Latin chapter titles with brief comments or summaries in English. This article was reprinted in the AFA *Bulletin* 11:5 (May 27, 1949), with additional notes by the editor.

Abu 'Ali's teacher Masha'allah (c.740-c.815) was the foremost of the early Arabian astrologers (he was actually a Jew). He was a prolific writer, and many of his books were translated into Latin. His name in Latin was Messahalla or some similar spelling. He was familiar with the *Pentateuch* of Dorotheus of Sidon (1st cent.), which

---

1. Extract from *The Fihrist of al-Nadim* edited and translated by Bayard Dodge (New York: Columbia Univ. Press, 1970), p. 655. See also Heinrich Suter, *Die Mathematiker und Astronomen der Araber und ihre Werke* (Leipzig: B.G. Teubner, 1900), pp. 9-10, and the *Encyclopedia of Islam* (Leiden: Brill, 1960-. 2nd. ed., in progress).
2. See Francis J. Carmody, *Arabic Astronomical and Astrological Sciences in Latin Translation* (Berkeley & Los Angeles: Univ. of Calif. Press, 1956).

became available in Arabic translation during his lifetime.[3] Carmody lists three books that he wrote on nativities. One of these has been edited by Pingree.[4] It consists of a short text of nine pages in Pingree's edition followed by twelve example horoscopes, of which three are taken from the *Pentateuch*. The text contains six chapters and the horoscopes. These chapters correspond to the first seven chapters of Abu 'Ali's book (Masha'allah's Chapt. 5 = Abu 'Ali's Chapts. 5 & 6) and the same twelve horoscopes. But Pingree's statement that "it is the basis of the main work of Masha'allah's pupil al-Khayyat"[5] is not supported by the evidence, since Abu 'Ali's text of Chapts. 1-7 is fuller and his book also contains 38 additional chapters not present in the text edited by Pingree. I have translated a few chapters of Masha'allah's work in Appendix 2. The reader can compare them with Abu 'Ali's text and form his own opinion.

It seems to me that Abu 'Ali, bearing in mind his teacher's instruction, used the same material for the early chapters of his book, thus producing a text similar to Masha'allah's, but not directly derived from it. In any case the influence of the *Pentateuch* is obvious. The use of the rulers of the triplicities as significators is characteristic of that work; also, the frequent use of the Parts and their rulers.

During the four centuries intervening between John of Seville's translation and its publication by Joachim Heller, Abu 'Ali was frequently quoted in the astrological literature, usually under the name "Albohali." In more recent times, he was cited by Jean Baptiste Morin (1583-1656) in his *Astrologia Gallica*.[6] It was this citation by Morin that first aroused my interest in Abu 'Ali. It seemed to me that although Morin disagreed with the Arab's use of triplicity rulers, he might well have found some of his other techniques more satisfactory.

Morin refers specifically to Abu 'Ali in Chapt. 7 of Book 21 of *Astrologia Gallica*,[7] where he contrasts Abu 'Ali's method of interpretation using rulers of the triplicities with his own method, which is more specific. And in fact Abu 'Ali does use house rulers extensively, in contrast to Ptolemy. However, unlike Ptolemy (and Morin), Abu 'Ali followed the standard Greek tradition in using Parts.[8]

---

3. See the edition by David Pingree, *Carmen astrologicum* (Leipzig: B.G. Teubner, 1976).

4. E.S. Kennedy and David Pingree, *The Astrological History of Masha'allah* (Cambridge, Mass.: Harvard Univ. Press, 1971), Appendix 3.

5. See his article on Masha'allah in the *Dictionary of Scientific Biography* (New York: Charles Scribner's Sons, 1970-80).

6. Published posthumously at The Hague in 1661.

7. See Richard S. Baldwin's translation (Washington: A.F.A., 1974.), pp. 72-73.

8. Parts or Lots are a common feature of Greek astrology. They are very old and evidently go back to the early writers. Modern astrologers, finding many of them mentioned in the Arabic writers but only one (The Part of Fortune) in Ptolemy, have supposed that they were invented by the Arabs; hence, they are usually termed "the Arabian Parts." The Arabs did invent many of their own, but they inherited a plentiful supply from the Greeks. Ptolemy himself remarks (*Tetrabiblos*, iii. 3) "What, however admits of prediction we shall investigate, not by means of lots and numbers of which no reasonable explanation can be given...." This allusion clearly shows that the writers known to

INTRODUCTION

Abu 'Ali's *Judgments of Nativities* could be described as a typical example of "Arabian" astrology. But it is more than that. It is an example of Greek astrology slightly modified and developed by the Arabian astrologers. For by and large, Arabian astrology is Greek astrology. This is especially true of natal astrology. In order to understand the reasons for this statement, it is necessary to consider the history of astrology.

The Family Tree of Astrology.

Horoscopic astrology originated in Alexandria, Egypt, in the second century B.C. as an amalgam of Babylonian, Greek, and Egyptian elements. The principal innovations were the system of celestial houses, classification and rulership of the signs, the aspects, and revised natures of the signs and planets. It is called Greek astrology because the original treatises and most of those that survive from the classical period were written in that language. (The Latin treatises of Manilius and Firmicus Maternus are the only exceptions.) It passed to the Hindus in the second century A.D. and to the Persians in the third century.

Ptolemaic Astrology.

In the second century A.D., Claudius Ptolemy wrote a small book on astrology. It is undoubtedly the most famous astrology book ever written and has excercised an influence on Western Astrology out of all proportion to its intrinsic merit. By the end of the third century, Ptolemy had come to be considered the premier astronomer and geographer of the classical world. Since he had also written a book on astrology, his fame spilled over into that field. As the centuries rolled on, his reputation grew, until some astrologers came to believe that he had actually invented astrology. (Obviously, those had not read his book attentively.)

The truth of the matter is that he was not an astrologer at all, but merely a science writer.⁹ He had already written a major book on astronomy (the *Syntaxis* or *Almagest*), so it was logical to write one on astrology. So far, so good. He evidently wanted to write something worthwhile, but he was obviously unwilling to devote the time and

---

Ptolemy used Lots as aids to interpretation.

9. He may not have been much of an astronomer either. See Robert R. Newton *The Crime of Claudius Ptolemy* (Baltimore & London: Johns Hopkins Univ. Press, 1977). Newton demonstrates that most of Ptolemy's astronomical "observations" were fictitious, that he tampered with the records of observations made by earlier astronomers, that he copied Hipparchus's Star Catalog (merely adding 2°40' to the longitudes), and that his mathematical treatment of planetary motions was not necessarily the best. Newton also declares that the public success of Ptolemy's astronomical works may have deprived us of works of equal or greater value by causing a loss of interest in them. I would extend his statement to include astrological works.

effort necessary to do the subject justice.[10]

He does not even pretend to set forth Greek astrology in full detail, for he says:

> "...we shall decline to present the ancient method of prediction, which brings into combination all or most of the stars, because it is manifold and well-nigh infinite, if one wishes to recount it with accuracy...and furthermore we shall omit it on account of the difficulty in using it and following it."[11]

Here are some of the things Ptolemy "declined to present":

1. The influences of the planets in the signs.

2. The influences of the planets in the houses.

3. The influences of the mutual aspects of the planets.

4. The method of using the Parts (other than the Part of Fortune)

5. The method of reading a chart by means of derived houses, house rulers, and dispositors.

He gives no example charts and mentions no astrologer by name.

The ancient method that he found so complicated and difficult is in fact quite similar to that used in Horary Astrology, which has been transmitted to us from the Greeks more or less intact only because Ptolemy chose to ignore it.

The rules and procedures of natal astrology set forth in the 3rd and 4th Books of the *Tetrabiblos* do not give an accurate picture of astrology as it existed in Ptolemy's day. He has largely ignored the houses and the accidental significators and substituted a simplistic method based upon universal significators and appearances. This method is "Ptolemaic Astrology." It is a deviant version of Greek Astrology, at variance with the teaching and practice of 2nd century astrologers.

Having mentioned some of the things Ptolemy left out of his version of astrology, it is important to see what additions and changes he made. He had already introduced a significant change in astronomy by adopting the vernal equinox as the First Point of Aries. He mentions this change in his astrological book,[12] and it became

---

10. William Lilly notes in his *Christian Astrology* (London: Partridge & Blunden, 1647), p. 553, that Ptolemy "in all his writings was extreame short."
11. *Tetrabiblos* (iii. 1) ed. and trans. by F.E.Robbins (Loeb Classical Library, 1940),
12. *Tetrabiblos*, i. 22, where he notes that "the writers [on astrology] make this quite clear" [that the equinox is the proper starting point].

standard in western astrology. His other main innovation was his
procedure for determining the length of life.[13]

His method of selecting the prorogator of life -- the *Hyleg*, as
the Arabs and their successors called it -- and of making
astronomical calculations to bring it into configuration with a fatal
point in the horoscope caught the fancy of succeeding generations of
astrologers. The Arabian astrologers give more elaborate rules for
the selection of the Hyleg than Ptolemy gave. Whether these were
their own or derived from the Persians ("Hyleg" is from a Persian
word) or from some late Greek source that passed through the Persians
to the Arabs is uncertain.

Astrology During the Middle Ages.

The Roman Empire was split in the fourth century. In that same
century Christianity became the state religion. It was hostile to
astrology (and to science and philosophy in general). In the fifth
century the Western empire collapsed. Europe entered a period of
stagnation, depression, and ignorance that lasted for seven
centuries. Public education died out. Public Libraries were pillaged.
Knowledge of the Greek language died out. Knowledge of the Latin
language died out except in the monasteries. Literacy retreated into
the monasteries. The monasteries copied books for their own use, but
the commercial book trade vanished (no customers!). The only
exception was Italy itself, where a thin stream of lay literacy and
education maintained itself during the dark ages. Under these
conditions, astrology all but died out.

In the Eastern Roman Empire, education, libraries, and the book
trade persisted. Library resources were drastically reduced with the
loss of the great collection at Alexandria and important collections
at other locations, but smaller collections remained at
Constantinople and elsewhere. Knowledge of Latin became rare, but
that was no great loss to science, for there never had been much
scientific or astrological literature in Latin. The intellectual
climate favored theology and opposed science and astrology as in the
West, but some astrological activity evidently persisted even in the
sixth and seventh centuries.

Hindu Astrology.

Greek astrology had found fertile soil in India. From the second
century A.D. forward the Hindus studied astronomy and astrology and
adapted both to their own ideas. The astrology (and astronomy) they
obtained from the West was pre-Ptolemaic. Consequently, the classical
Hindu astrology preserves features of the older Greek astrology, such
as the use of the Sign-House system of house division, the

---

13. *Tetrabiblos*, iii. 10. This chapter has sparked interminable arguments among astrologers and
led to the invention of the two principal modern systems of house division, those of Regiomontanus
and Placidus, each of whom claimed to have determined "the true method of Ptolemy."

calculation of aspects by whole signs rather than by degrees, and the use of a fixed zodiac. The principal native element added was the system of *nakshatras* or Lunar Mansions.

Persian Astrology.

The Persians studied astronomy and astrology, particularly Mundane Astrology, and composed treatises on it prior to the forced Islamization of the country in the seventh century. Fanatic Arabs destroyed most of the Persian literature on all subjects, so not much is known about individual writers or their books, but some books on astronomy and astrology survived long enough to be translated into Arabic in the eighth and ninth centuries.

How Astrology Came to the Arabs.

The Arabs were theoretically opposed to astrology. Mohammed had said in the Koran, "The astrologers are liars, by the Lord of the Kaaba!" But the craving for knowledge ultimately proved stronger than strict orthodoxy. By the end of the eighth century, the Arabs had become seekers of knowledge of all sorts. They soon discovered that the Byzantine Empire was a storehouse of information on everything under the sun. A steady stream of Greek books began to flow into Baghdad and other centers of learning. These were translated into Arabic and made available to the public.

There were also Greek, Persian, and Hindu astrologers at court in Baghdad. Their presence gave impetus to the acquisition and translation of astrological literature from their languages. The Arabs obtained the works of Dorotheus, Ptolemy, Vettius Valens, Antiochus of Athens, and other Greek writers. Arabic translations of some Middle Persian and Sanskrit astrological texts were also made, but the contributions from these two languages are most apparent in Mundane astrology. To these foreign elements, the Arabs added their own traditional lore on the 28 Mansions of the Moon and some of the other fixed stars.

Arabian Astrology.

Arabian astrology is the name given to the works of the medieval astrologers who wrote in the Arabic language in the period from about 790 to 1170 A.D. The writers were mostly Arabs, but a few were Jews or Persians. Many of their books were translated into Latin by the so-called "twelfth century translators." These translations formed the basis of European astrological knowledge and the foundation of the modern tradition.

In the case of Natal astrology, Arabian astrology is essentially classical Greek astrology with an admixture of Ptolemaic astrology. This Greek mixture was modified and extended by the Arab astrologers in the light of their own experience and social conditions, but the changes are minor. The obvious differences, then, between Arabian natal astrology and Ptolemaic natal astrology are not due to "Arabian influence," as modern astrologers have almost universally supposed, but to the fact that Ptolemaic natal astrology is a deviant offshoot of traditional Greek natal astrology. It is Ptolemy that is peculiar, not the Arabs.

The important point to note is that when you read Arabian natal astrology, the basis of what you are reading is traditional Greek astrology, interspersed here and there with Ptolemaic astrology, but still essentially traditional.

Astrology in the Renaissance and Early Modern Period.

The great thirteenth century European astrologers, such as Guido Bonatti, practiced Arabian astrology. This was also true of their successors in the two succeeding centuries, but the recovery of Greek learning in the West cast an aura of superiority over everything Greek. This caused astrologers to pay more attention to Ptolemy's *Quadripartite (Tetrabiblos)* as an individual work of merit. Previously they had been content to use Ptolemy as cited by the Arabs in their books, although the complete book had been available in a Latin version translated from the Arabic since the twelfth century.

Once the *Quadripartite* was read by itself, the astrologers were struck by the numerous differences between it and the works of the Arabic astrologers. Knowing little or nothing of the history of astrology, they naturally supposed that the differences they saw were "inventions of the Arabs." Partly due to the enthusiasm for anything Greek, and partly due to political and religious prejudice against the Muslim states, there was a movement away from Arabian Astrology toward Ptolemaic Astrology.

We may summarize the changing attitudes of astrologers during the succeeding centuries down to the present as follows. A few astrologers tried to adopt a strictly Ptolemaic form of astrology. This was of course impossible, since Ptolemaic astrology is too skimpy to use effectively by itself. Another group stuck with the (Arabian) tradition but paid more attention to the Ptolemaic features. And a third group ignored Ptolemaic astrology as a separate kind of astrology and continued to use the tradition as before.

Horary Astrology vs. Natal Astrology.

The principal branches of astrology are Horary, Natal, and Mundane. Horary answers questions and only requires a clock and a current ephemeris. Natal requires a knowledge of the latitude and longitude of the birthplace, the exact date of birth, the time of birth to at least the nearest hour, and an ephemeris (or planetary tables) for the birthyear. It may also require a knowledge of calendar conversions if the clients are from foreign places. We are not concerned here with Mundane, so we will skip over its requirements.

Horary Astrology answers the question of the moment. Natal Astrology gives a general account of the entire life of a client. Some astrologers practice one or the other exclusively, some both. In classical antiquity and the Middle Ages there does not seem to have been any thought that one branch was superior to the other -- they were simply used for different purposes. However, when astrologers began to divide up over Ptolemaic Astrology, they noticed that Ptolemy's *Tetrabiblos* was restricted to Natal (and Mundane) Astrology. So another wrong idea arose: Natal Astrology was Ptolemaic, but Horary Astrology must have been invented by the Arabs.

Another three-way split in attitudes developed. Some astrologers gave up Horary Astrology altogether (declaring it to be a wicked and valueless invention of the heathen Arabs) and practiced only Natal. Another group continued to practice both. And a third group practiced both or countenanced the practice of both, but insisted upon a different set of rules for each branch. This last group reasoned thus: Ptolemaic Astrology, which was (so they supposed) the pure, original form of Natal Astrology, did not use house rulers and other features of Horary Astrology; therefore, these features were inappropriate for Natal Astrology and must be used exclusively in Horary Astrology. The fact that this attitude was inherently illogical does not seem to have bothered its supporters.

To sum up, Arabian Astrology is Greek Astrology with an admixture of Ptolemaic Astrology. It was popular in the Middle Ages and the Renaissance, but acquired a bad name (for a wrong reason) in the Early Modern period. This bad name caused a reaction in favor of pure Ptolemaic Astrology and a schism between the techniques of Natal Astrology and Horary Astrology that has persisted to the present day.

Abu 'Ali's *Judgments of Nativities*

Back now to Abu 'Ali. His book on nativities is in the main stream of the Arabian tradition. It is, therefore, very different from the *Tetrabiblos*. The principal differences are the use of the Lord of the Time, triplicity rulers, houses as primary sources of signification, house rulers, dispositors, special rules for strength and weakness of planetary rulers, and concurrent use of special Parts for judgment of specific matters. There is emphasis on reinforcement of indications by two or more horoscopic indications. Some of the techniques are unfamiliar to modern astrologers and therefore offer opportunities for research.

I would like to point out some features of the book. First, it is not a beginner's book. As we saw above, Abu 'Ali had written an *Introduction* to astrology, and he would have presumed that those who took up his *Judgments of Nativities* would have already mastered the fundamentals. Consequently, he does not usually define the technical terms he uses, nor does he think it necessary to explain how to calculate the "Parts" he mentions. I have added footnotes where I thought the modern reader might need some help.

Another important point. Abu 'Ali seems to have used what we call the Equal House method of house division.[14] In this system, the degree of the ASC is the cusp of the 1st house, and the cusps of the other houses are found by successively adding 30° to it. Thus, if the degree of the ASC is 15 Taurus, then the cusp of the 2nd house is 15 Gemini, the cusp of the 3rd house is 15 Cancer, and so on. In this system, the midheaven or MC is always 90° behind the degree of the ASC, 15 Aquarius in the example just given.

But underlying this system of houses is another more ancient system that I have called "Sign-House."[15] In this method, which is still in use to some extent in India, the rising sign is determined. Then, it is considered to be the 1st house, the next sign the 2nd house, etc. Degrees do not enter into it. Or, to put it another way, the cusp is invariably at the beginning of the sign. In the example previously used, Taurus would be the 1st house, Gemini the 2nd house, etc. Thus, Abu 'Ali speaks indifferently of the "8th house" or the "8th sign."

In both of these systems, each house consists of exactly 30°. There are no "intercepted signs" as with the various systems of unequal house division. Nor does the same sign appear on more than one cusp. This point is especially noted by Joachim Heller in the Introduction to the Latin edition.

The reader will also note that the author frequently adds "of the circle (of houses)" to the number of the house, as "Mars in the 8th house of the circle." This is an ancient usage which reflects the fact that the originators of astrology were accustomed to count houses not just from the ASC, but also from the Sun, the Moon, the Part of Fortune, one of the other Parts, or a planet. The primary ring of houses is of course that of the "circle of houses" anchored on the ASC, and the reader can assume that that is what is meant if no other starting point is specified.

Those who are accustomed to one of the unequal methods of house division may suppose that the Sign-House and Equal House methods are primitive and inadequate. Not necessarily so. House division has been a topic of contention among astrologers ever since the so-called "Porphyry" system was devised (2nd century?). It has not yet been satisfactorily resolved. The reader who wishes to test the methods of interpretation given in this book is advised to try the old methods of house division as well as whichever one of the unequal systems he is accustomed to using.

I also call the reader's attention to an important point stressed by the Arabian author. Astrology works within the bounds of the possible. It is most unlikely that the son of a peasant will become

---

14. Seven of the corresponding charts in the text of Masha'allah's *Book of Nativities* have Alchabitius cusps. But it is perhaps noteworthy that in four out of the five cases where Abu 'Ali has given the ASC degree, Masha'allah's chart has a different ASC degree. Figures of any sort are prone to error, but this looks like deliberate alteration. If so, then the (astronomical) MC degree and the intermediate cusps may have been added to Masha'allah's charts by some copyist or redactor.

15. See my paper "Ancient House Division" in the *Journal of Research* of the AFA, vol. 1, no. 1 (1982).

king or acquire great wealth or become a learned professor. The astrologer must consider the native's origins and circumstances before rendering judgment. This has always been a fundamental tenet of astrology, but it is sometimes forgotten by astrologers who are used to dealing with clients of the same social class in a single country.

The reader must also realize that a 9th century astrologer read the charts of nobles, merchants, scholars, ecclesiastics, military leaders, certain skilled artisans, and their children. He seldom or never read the charts of poor people. Few of them would have known their birthdates, much less their birth times,[16] nor would they have had money to pay for professional services. Slaves, perhaps, because some slaves had seen better days. Ditto captives. But the few references that seem to imply that horoscopes were or had been read for the poor probably heark back to Classical times when literacy was more widespread, and when even a poor man might know his birth data.

The references to the "art of writing" and the "art of arithmetic" are a tipoff to the state of medieval society. A man who could read and write and do a little simple arithmetic had a fine general education in the 9th century. Not that there were no persons of greater accomplishments, but they were extremely few. As always, astrology reflects the social conditions of the society in which it is practised.

Finally, I must note a difference between the way that Abu 'Ali presents his interpretations of a position or a configuration. He typically gives the **maximum** effect that can be expected from the position. This differs considerably from the 20th century practice of stating an **average** effect or even a "psychological tendency." But the author states quite clearly that many factors have to be present to produce the maximum effect. He explains what those factors are, and he expects his reader to follow his method, not to assume the maximum effect from a single unsupported position. (This is the fundamental mistake made by modern "researchers" who diligently tabulate the house positions or sign positions of planets without any further consideration, and who therefore come up with little or nothing to show for their effort.)

Now, read the Latin Editor's Introduction, which follows this, and then read Abu 'Ali's book from beginning to end. I believe you will find it interesting.

James H. Holden

May 20, 1988.

---

16. There is an amusing incident in the *Arabian Nights* where a teen-age girl has to go ask her mother for her birthdate so that she can consult an astrologer, but the mother can only recall that the girl was born on the same night that a famous local citizen had accidentally disgraced himself at his wedding feast. This illustrates how the dates of events were sometimes remembered in those days.

TO HIS TEACHER,

THE VERY FAMOUS AND LEARNED

PHILIP MELANCHTHON,

Joachim Heller of Weissenfels

With the Greatest Respect

Gives Special Greeting.

Long ago, Most Learned Teacher,[1] I prayed to God, the Best and
Greatest, that eventually some testimony of my gratitude and
everlasting respect for you would come to public notice. By some
peculiar chance beyond my hope and expectation it has happened, both
quickly and as I hope, happily enough. There fell into my hands an
old manuscript of admirable antiquity containing some commentaries on
celestial matters. This manuscript, which formerly belonged to the
library of that magnanimous and glorious hero, Matthew, King of
Hungary,[2] escaped by no less happy a fate than by that singular (as I
indeed interpret it) genius of our city, which constantly favors this
most beautiful part of philosophy, and was preserved until now and
finally brought to me to be sold. In it there are several treatises
of the old astrologers, and also the one which now for the first time
appears in public under the auspices of your famous name, that of the
Arabian Astrologer.

May you accept then, Dearest Teacher, an ancient book not
previously edited, but short and written in an humble style, not
indeed because it might seem to be a worthy gift for such a patron,
but because it was made by me. For I would rather seize this
occasion, such as it is, for declaring my good will towards you, than
pursue the hope of a greater gratitude. And I ask most earnestly that
you pardon me in my love and zeal for you.

---

1. According to Lynn Thorndike (HMES, V, 337, 365, 394-6), Joachim Heller (c.1518-c.1590)
studied at Wittenberg under the famous Reformation scholar and theologian Philip Melanchthon (1497-
1560), who was professor of Greek and a life-long advocate of astrology.
2. Matthias Corvinus (c.1443-1490). He was a life-long book-collector, who founded a magnificent
library in Buda (now part of Budapest). The library was sacked by the Turks in 1526, and many of
the books were carried off to Constantinople, but some were seized by individual soldiers, who
disposed of them locally.

There are, furthermore, other causes which led me to do this:
first, because it was very well known to me, that you, Most Learned
Sir, especially delight in this kind of learning; and second, that by
your judgment and vote of approval you are accustomed to bestow as
much dignity and authority on this art, as besides you few, and only
the greatest artists have conferred upon these divine studies.

For it is not unknown to you how great is the perversity and
iniquity of the vulgar judgments by which these studies, which were
not revealed and disclosed to excellent talents except by some divine
command, are derided and condemned in the extreme. But these new men,
partly impious and partly ignorant, accomplish nothing if they spurn
God's most outstanding gifts and afflict them with insults. Pious and
holy minds acknowledge and highly esteem these great benefactions of
God, conceded to mankind because of their very great utility in life,
and with their own ears and minds they shrink away from those
tasteless and Epicurean outcries of the mob.

Truly, since you have already seriously and copiously discussed
these matters for the vindication of true philosophy, we may revert
to the discourse given by our author. He has a method in common with
the rest of the Arabs, Hindus, and Persians, who for many centuries
back have made use of the teachings of this divine philosophy, in the
judgments of which it is permitted to detect precisely this order:

They begin by looking at the cusp of the particular house (as they
say), and they consider the bodies and the rays of the fortunate as
well as the malefic stars on it through the mean value of their own
discovered orbs. After that, they also consider the lord of the sign
that is on the cusp of the house, diligently observing its nature as
well as its position in the circle--strong or weak--and the mutual
configurations of the fortunes or infortunes with it.

In addition to this, they consider the universal or natural
significator of each house, and of the thing quesited, whether they
are strong or weak, both essentially and in mundo. These are the more
powerful and universal decrees and testimonies.

But having set these aside, they have recourse to those weaker,
but not absolutely ineffectual significations of the Parts.
Especially if some indications agree--the votes of the fortunate
stars, or conversely the adverse impediments of the unfavorable
stars. In addition, they also look at the lords of the Parts, and
their strengths and weaknesses. And they diligently ponder their
houses and applications, just as they do with the rest of the
significators.

And finally, they also take into consideration, that which is most
powerful for ascertaining the time of events--the lords of the
triplicity of the domicile, i.e. of the celestial sign, whose decrees
they are investigating in the horoscope. And to all this they add
certain rules, approved by the long experience of the ages. This,
more or less, is the method, which the present author also observes
most diligently.

It is also noteworthy that he everywhere retains the equal
intervals of the twelve houses of heaven in the zodiac, which both
Ptolemy and the oldest teachers of celestial things followed.[3] For
how much confusion is there both of order and also of the influences
themselves, whenever three signs at a time, according to the
inventions of the modern writers,[4] flow together into the same
house?[5] Or when a single sign, the others having been shoved aside as
it were, often occupies three houses of heaven?[6] How much these
things differ from the ancient systems and from the precepts of the
wise men, the facts and the writings of earlier ages speak for
themselves. For if you follow the moderns, the most diverse and
plainly contrary decrees of the same house often occur, because of
the different signs coming together in it. Or, if you give preference
to the sign that appears on the cusp, the others must necessarily
remain non-signifying.[7] Or, the influences of different houses will
be precisely the same, whenever a sign taking the beginning in
anything is extended through three cusps.

So obstinately do they pursue this, that they make the influences
of the zodiac dependent upon the rule of the *primum mobile*, so that
they also either throw these decrees of the influences into absolute
disorder or they very nearly tear them away from the circle. And well
indeed this scheme might have succeeded for them, if they had
transferred the fixed as well as the wandering stars, placed in the
solar path, there along with the luminaries themselves.

But I ask you, what difference does it make in these influences of
heaven, whether the degrees of the zodiac move obliquely or directly?
Why do all the philosophers affirm that the obliquity of this circle
is the cause of all changes, of all generation and corruption in
inferior things and bodies? And this certainly not by itself, but
because of the varied motions and concourses of the luminaries and
planets that take place in it.

Why don't they transfer these same effects (if to be sure it is
pleasing to demolish and reject the findings of the ancients and all
the fundamentals of the art), along with the names of the signs, to
this same parallel of the equinoxes? For then the rising and setting
of the circle would be uniform. Then they could describe and divide
equal spaces of houses deduced from the poles of the world. And there

---

3. Despite assertions to the contrary by many subsequent writers, the natural sense of the words
Ptolemy uses in *Tetrabiblos* iii. 10 (Sect. 128) is that he is speaking of the Equal House system.
4. The reference is to the use of the system of houses devised by Regiomontanus (1436-1476),
whose tables were first published in 1490. In this system, the equator was divided equally, but the
ecliptic was not.
5. That is, when a sign is intercepted in a house, the house actually contains all of one sign
and parts of the two adjacent signs.
6. Here, Heller refers to the opposite situation from that just mentioned. That is, when a sign
begins in one house, extends all the way across the next house, and occupies a portion of the next
house after that. This is as bad as it gets in Nürnberg and in lower latitudes, but from Lat. 52°
northward it becomes worse, for it is possible in such high latitudes for the same sign to appear
on three successive cusps.
7. Translating the Greek word *Asemos* in Heller's text.

would be no confusion and inequality in the division of the houses.[8]

Truly, Nature herself (as I have said), who has surrounded and decorated the circle of influences with many conspicuous stars, opposes this. The motions of the planets, which turn aside their courses not at the equator, but at the boundaries of the zodiac, also oppose. Those planets whose congresses and configurations with the stars contained within this circle, Experience, the teacher of celestial things, very clearly teaches and demonstrates to have marvelous effects.

Therefore, let the *equator*[9] be the Measure of the *primum mobile* and the distributor of times, not the Regulator (so to speak) of the signs of the zodiac,[10] the use of which also for the word "houses" this author too, as well as others, testifies that the ancients have employed.[11]

The ecliptic can by a quite similar procedure (just as we have received the tradition from the first inventors of the art) be divided into twelve equal parts by circles deduced from its poles. The influences and the celestial motions and the writings of antiquity support this--the consensus then of Nature herself. Truly, these things have been proved with most learned and certain reasons and testimonies by the very learned Johann Schöner.[12] Having been so warned, I want the reader to observe in these old examples what method of division of the houses of heaven the ancients observed.

But I also beg of you, Most Learned Teacher, that you kindly accept this worthless trifle of gratitude, sent to you in Schöner's name as well as in mine. Because if we understand that you approve our work in this field, we shall undertake to communicate [to you] Albumasar (whose text we have noticed in many places differs very much from the earliest manuscript) both fuller from additions that are not to be spurned and corrected in many places by scholars, and anything else that we may judge would be profitable for common studies.[13]

---

8. In other words, why not transfer the signs to the equator and eliminate the problem? (Heller is speaking sarcastically.)

9. Translating the Greek word *isemerinos* in Heller's text.

10. He means, let the equator be used to establish time measures, but not to establish the cusps of the houses, which lie in the zodiacal circle.

11. That is, the word "sign" is frequently used as an equivalent term for "(celestial) house."

12. Johann Schöner (1477-1547) was professor of mathematics at Nürnberg 1526-1546 (Thorndike, *op. cit.*, V, 354 ff, 394). He was also a student of astrology and astronomy and published a considerable number of works on both subjects from 1515 on. Two years before his death, he published a major work on nativities *De judiciis nativitatum libri tres* (Nürnberg: J. Montanus and U. Neuber, 1545). He had favored the Regiomontanus system of house division in his earlier writings, but perhaps in the book just mentioned he argued in favor of a return to Equal House and Sign-House.

13. Thorndike observes (*op. cit.*, V, 395) that Heller does not seem to have ever published anything by Albumasar, but this may be because his elder colleague Schöner died the next year. He did however publish John of Seville's *Epitome totius Astrologiae* in 1548 and several of Masha'allah's numerous works in 1549.

And we in turn urge you and beseech you publicly in the name of all that you furnish us at last a complete version of Ptolemy's *Tetrabiblos* with your learned commentary.[14] For we are confident that it will be done so clearly that these divine studies of celestial things will recoup their former light and dignity. Which, we implore and entreat you most reverently to do.

Farewell, O Philip, Ornament of Letters and of True Religion,[15] and may good fortune be yours.

From that famous Nürnberg, Germany.

April 1, 1546.

---

14. Melanchthon eventually complied with this request. His edition of the Greek text of the *Tetrabiblos* with a Latin translation was published at Basel in 1553. Thorndike (*op. cit.*, V, 400) says Joachim Camerarius (1500-1574) translated the first two books and Melanchthon translated the last two. The following year, he published an edition of Proclus's *Paraphrase* of the *Tetrabiblos* (*Procli paraphrasis...* Basel: J. Oporinum, [1554]).

15. Melanchthon was an intimate friend of Martin Luther (1483-1546) and the leading scholar of the Reformation. (He edited Luther's translation of the Bible into German.) Following Luther's death, he became the acknowledged leader of the Reformation in Germany.

ABU 'ALI AL-KHAYYAT

JUDGMENTS OF NATIVITIES.

Preface.

Abu 'Ali said, "This is the book in which I have set forth and collected all the significations on nativities of the science of judgments of the stars which ought not to be ignored by any master of this great and lofty science, the certitude of which, with God's help, we shall disclose briefly and simply."

Chapt. 1. *Rearing [of Children].*

First of all, it is necessary to know in advance the knowledge of rearing, for which you ought to consider the lords of the triplicity[1] of the ASC, and the lords of the triplicity of the Sun by day, [and the lords of the triplicity of the Moon by night],[2] and the lords of the triplicity of the Sun by day [or of the Moon by night] of the sign of the New Moon or the Full Moon[3] that was before the nativity, also Jupiter and Venus, and the diurnal planets if the nativity was diurnal, and the nocturnal planets if the nativity was nocturnal.

And you will begin with the lords of the triplicity of the ASC, that is to say the first and second lords. And if one of them is in the ASC, or the MC, or the 11th, or the 4th house,[4] free from impediments and from malefic stars, it signifies good rearing, if God is willing.

But if both of them are cadent and impedited by the evil [stars],[5] look at the lords of the triplicity of the Sun if it is a diurnal nativity, or the lords of the triplicity of the Moon if it is a

---

1. According to Dorotheus, the lords of of the triplicities are as follows. Fire: by day, Sun, Jupiter, and Saturn; by night, Jupiter, Sun, and Saturn. Earth: by day, Venus, the Moon, and Mars; by night, the Moon, Venus, and Mars. Air: by day, Saturn, Mercury, and Jupiter; by night, Mercury, Saturn, and Jupiter. Water: by day, Venus, Mars, and the Moon; by night, Mars, Venus, and the Moon.
2. This and the following addition seem called for, since they are part of the rules specified in the third and fifth paragraphs below.
3. The Latin text consistently has *coniunctio* 'conjunction' and *praeventio* 'anticipation' for the conjunction and opposition of the Sun and Moon. To make the English translation more understandable, I have used the familiar terms "New Moon" and "Full Moon."
4. The Latin has *loco* 'place', which was the original term for one of the twelve segments of the horoscope, but modern terminology requires 'house'.
5. The Latin often uses the adjectives 'bad' or 'good' without expressing the noun 'stars' (i.e., 'planets'). This usage is restricted in English, so I have added the appropriate noun in brackets.

nocturnal nativity. If they are in good signs, free from impediments
and from the [aspects of] the infortunes, they signify rearing.

But if these too are impedited and in bad houses, look at the
lords of the triplicity of the Part of Fortune.⁶ If they are in good
houses, free from impediments, and the Sun aspects the Part of
Fortune in diurnal nativities, or the Moon in nocturnal nativities,
they signify rearing.

But if these are impedited and are in evil houses, consider the
lords of the triplicity of the sign of the New Moon, if of course the
nativity was a New Moon nativity, or the sign of the Full Moon if the
Full Moon preceded [the nativity]. If they are in angles or in
succedents of the angles, attacked by no impediments or rays of the
malefics, they signify rearing.

But if they are impedited and in evil houses, look at Jupiter or
Venus, because if one of them is in an angle or a succedent of an
angle, free from [aspects of] the evil [stars] and from impediments,
it signifies rearing.

But if both are impedited and in evil houses, look at the Moon. If
it is free from malefics and impediments, and there is a diurnal
planet in the ASC or in the MC in diurnal nativities or a nocturnal
planet in nocturnal nativities, it signifies rearing.

And if you find the Moon either impedited or located in an
unsuitable house, consider which planet has the greater signification
from among the lords of the triplicity of the ASC, and the triplicity
of the Sun by day and the Moon by night, and the triplicity of the
Part of Fortune, and the triplicity of the sign of the New Moon or
the Full Moon--the one [of them] to be sure which most nearly
preceded the nativity. If they are in angles or succedents of angles,
free from [the aspects of] evil stars and impediments, it signifies
rearing. And if they are impedited and in evil houses, they signify
little rearing, and impediment, and a brief span of life.

And the native will live as long as the number of degrees that is
between the planet which is Almuten⁷ over the native and the evil
[stars] in days, months, or years. In short, in similar fashion, if
the Almuten over the native is cadent, and the degree of the ASC and
the Moon are applied to⁸ evil [stars], the native will live according
to the number of degrees which is between the degree of the ASC and
the evil [stars] [that many] days, months, or years.

In the same manner, if the degree of the Sun or the Moon [is] in
conjunction, or in square, or in opposite aspect to an infortune, and
there are few degrees between them, the native will live for [so
many] days, months, or years according to the number of degrees which

---

6. Abu 'Ali assumes the reader knows how to calculate this Part. The formula is Moon - Sun + ASC
by day, and Sun - Moon + ASC by night.
7. The Latin text has *almutez*, which is nearly correct (the Arabic word is *al-mubtazz* 'one who
has gotten the better of someone'), but the corrupted spelling *almuten* has become established in
the literature. The Almuten is the strongest planet and hence the ruler over whatever is specified.
8. Or perhaps, 'close to'.

is between them. Similarly, if the Lord of Time, namely the luminary in authority,[9] is found in conjunction, or square, or opposite aspect to the malefics, it signifies a brief life unless a strong fortune aspects it.

And if the Moon is besieged between two malefics, of which one is in the ASC and the other is in the 7th house of heaven, and especially when there is a malefic close to one of the angles, and the Moon is impeded in one of the angles, it signifies a short space of time. Furthermore, when the lords of the triplicity of the ASC, the Sun, the Moon, the Part of Fortune, and the sign of the New Moon or the Full Moon are impeded in whatever manner, in addition to being cadent from the angles, they signify rearing, but not without hard work and difficulty.

And when the first and second lords of the triplicity of the ASC are cadent from the angles and are also otherwise impedited, they signify a short duration of life of the native, especially if Saturn is in an angle in nocturnal nativities or Mars in diurnal [nativities]. But if the Moon is received, it signifies goodness of rearing, and the benevolence of men towards him, and many brothers and allies and friends. And if it is not received, it signifies the contrary. Also, when the Part of Fortune is with the Moon, and Venus aspects her in nocturnal nativities or Jupiter in diurnal nativities, it signifies good rearing, and especially if the Part is in a good house.

And so, when the planet that signifes rearing is oriental and in a masculine sign in diurnal nativities, or occidental and in a feminine sign in a nocturnal nativity, its strength will be greater and its testimony as to good rearing more veracious. And when the ASC and its lord is impeded, and the Moon and its lord, it signifies a brief and fleeting life and a rapid death. And this will occur especially in that time when in a [particular] year the profection of the year[10] comes to an angle where there is one of the malefics.

But if the native emerges from his first year, and you see [that he has] a nativity that signifies a short duration of life, you will direct the sign ascending to the conjunction, square, or opposition of the unfavorable stars, giving to each sign a month; and if this time too goes past one year, then it will be the sign of death. And make for yourself a testimony of the goodness of food and rearing from the fifth sign and its lord, and from the place of the Moon on the third day and the seventh [day] from the nativity.[11] For from the good fortune or impediment of these [places] is known the goodness or the destruction of rearing, and its increase or descrease, if God is willing.

---

9. More commonly called the "Light of (the) Time."
10. An ancient method of prediction set forth, for example, by Paul of Alexandria in his *Introduction to Astrology*, Chapt. 31. See also William Lilly's *Christian Astrology*, pp. 715-733. The yearly profection begins with the ASC and moves forward in the zodiac 30° per year, thus performing a revolution in 12 years. Refer to the sources just mentioned for technical details of its use.
11. Or as we would say, on the 2nd and 6th days after birth. (The ancients counted the birthday as 1, the next day as 2, etc.)

Chapt. 2. *The Hyleg and the Knowledge of the Length of Life.*

When you have found that the native will be reared, and you want to know the length of his life, seek out the Hyleg,[12] beginning with the Sun in diurnal nativities. If it is in an angle or a succedent of an an angle in a masculine sign, or in a masculine quarter, and if the lord of its domicile[13] or the lord of its term or the lord of its exaltation or the lord of its triplicity or face aspects it, then it can be the Hyleg.

And the Sun cannot be the Hyleg, nor can any other planet, unless one of the lords of the five essential dignities[14] aspects it, and this is a judgment that must always be observed with the Hyleg.

But if the Sun is not [eligible to be] the Hyleg, in the aforesaid manner, look at the Moon. If it is in an angle or a succedent of an angle, or in a feminine sign or in a feminine quarter, and anyone of the lords of the five dignities previously mentioned aspects it, it will be the Hyleg. But if the Moon is [situated] in some other manner, it will not be the Hyleg. Then, if it is a New Moon nativity, seek out the Hyleg from the ASC, just as you have sought it from the Sun and the Moon.

Next, if it cannot be the Hyleg, seek out the Hyleg from the Part of Fortune. But if it doesn't work out either, then seek out the Hyleg similarly from the one of those [stars] that was most dignified in the degree of the conjunction or opposition of the luminaries that was before the nativity.

In nocturnal nativities, begin with the Moon. If it is in an angle or a succedent of an angle, in a feminine sign, or in a feminine quarter, and one of the lords of the five dignities aspects it, it will be the Hyleg. But if it is not as we have said nor sufficiently fit to be the Hyleg, seek out the Hyleg from the Sun. If it is in an angle or a succedent of an angle, in a masculine sign, or in a masculine quarter, and one of the lords of the five dignities aspects it, it will be the Hyleg. But if it is less fit for the dignity of Hyleg, and it was a Full Moon nativity, seek out the Hyleg from the Part of Fortune. But if it was not fit to be the Hyleg, select the degree of the New Moon or the Full Moon that most nearly preceded the nativity. If it was in an angle or a succedent of an angle, and one of the lords of the five essential dignities aspects it, it will be the Hyleg.

---

12. The Latin spelling here is *hylech* -- from the Arabic *hilaj* from the Middle Pers. *hilak* 'let loose' which is a literal translation of the Grk. *aphetes*. This is a planet or point in the ecliptic that is "set free" to move by the diurnal motion until it encounters another planet or point that is considered to be fatal. Thus, the "Hyleg" is the prorogator that governs the life of the native.
13. The Latin word *domus* 'house' is used indifferently by this author to mean 'house (of heaven)' or 'sign'. In the translation I have translated the former meaning as 'house' and the latter as 'domicile'. Abu 'Ali occasionally uses the word *signum* 'sign', so the reader will be able to see the distinction.
14. That is, a planet that is ruler of the domicile, exaltation, term, triplicity, or face of the sign in which the planet under consideration is posited.

But when the Sun is the Hyleg, and it does not have an Alcochoden,[15] seek out the Hyleg from the degree of the New Moon or Full Moon which was before the nativity. Finally, if none of these [potential] Hylegs has an Alcochoden, the native will be frail and will live only a short time.

Nevertheless, it must be noted that when you have selected the ASC, or the Part of Fortune, or the degree of the conjunction or opposition, you don't care whether it is in masculine or feminine signs (because it is good in all signs), but you will consider whether it is in an angle or a succedent of an angle. And when the Part of Fortune is the Hyleg, you will not seek out an Alcochoden other than the lord of the domicile, or of the exaltation, or of the term.

Chapt. 3. *The Alcochoden and What it Signifies About Life.*

When you have determined the Hyleg and you want to know the Alcochoden, look at the lord of the term of the Hyleg, and the lord of its domicile, and the lord of its exaltation, or its triplicity, or its face. And if one of these aspects the Hyleg, that one is the Alcochoden; and if two or three or all of them aspect it, the one that has the most dignities and is closest to it in degrees will be the Alcochoden. But if there is one having the most dignities in the place of the Hyleg and closest to it in degrees, but it does not aspect the Hyleg, we shall take first the one nearest to it in the strength of its dignities (so long as it aspects the Hyleg), and that one will be the Alcochoden.

And know that when the Sun is allotted the Hylegiacal dignity and it is in Aries or Leo and none of the lords of the five dignities aspect it, it will be both Hyleg and Alcochoden. And similarly too, the Moon, when it is in Cancer or Taurus, and none of the lords of the five dignities of the sign it is in aspect it, it will be both Hyleg and Alcochoden.

And when you have recognized the Alcochoden, see if it is in an angle in its own domicile or exaltation or triplicity, oriental and free from [any aspect of] the evil [stars], and free from retrogradation and combustion, [for then] it signifies its own greater years for the native. And if they are in [houses] following the angles, similar to the situation just mentioned in the angles, it denotes its medium years for the native. But if it is in [houses that are] cadent from the angles, with those conditions which we have mentioned in the angles, it bestows its lesser years.

---

15. This term is spelled in a variety of ways in Latin and English. It is a transliteration of the Arabic *al-kadkhudah* from a Middle Persian phrase used to translate the Greek *oikodespotes* 'house-ruler' or simply 'ruler'. Wilson (*Dict. of Astrol.*) defines it as "an Arabic name for the Hyleg," but this is incorrect. It is actually the one of the "lords of the five dignities" that is in aspect with the Hyleg. It thus becomes a sort of joint ruler of the life of the native, as is explained below in Chapt. 3.

Furthermore, it ought to be known that however much the Alcochoden is diminished in its own convenience, strength, and dignity according to its place in the circle, or also through the applications of the stars, by just so much is the order of its own signification diminished. And when it is not oriental, it will be converted. And know that if the Alcochoden is diminished [in effectiveness] by any of these ways which I have recited, it will reduce its years according to its place in the circle in the manner which I shall state.

For when it is in an angle (but as I have said, with the exception that it is not oriental), it is converted from its greater to its medium years. And if it is occidental and peregrine, it descends from its medium to its minor years. And if it is occidental, peregrine, retrograde, and combust, it is converted from its minor years and months to a similar amount of months and days.[16] And you will observe this similarly with other impediments of the planets and with other houses of the circle, because it is a rule. And know that the Dragon's Head of the Moon, when it is before or after it, will increase by a fourth part the years which it signifies, and the closer it is to it in degrees, the better it will be. But when the Tail is in in its place, it will reduce by a fourth part the years which the Alcochoden signifies, and the closer it is to it, the worse it will be, and especially if the Sun or the Moon is the Alcochoden (and the Moon suffers more harm from it). Thus Ptolemy said that the Head with the planets increases, and the Tail reduces, but moreso with the Moon.[17] And if the Alcochoden is so placed that it signifies a short life, and Jupiter and Venus are in the ASC or the MC, there will be hope that the native will live as much longer as the quantity of their lesser years, unless the term of the ASC and the Moon is impedited by the evil [stars], or the one of the fortunes that signified life is the ruler of the House of Death, because then a short space of time and a swift death is signified.

---

16. The Latin text twice has *qualitas* 'quality' in error for *quantitas* 'quantity'.

17. Not in the *Tetrabiblos* or the *Centiloquy*, but perhaps in one of the numerous spurious works attributed to Ptolemy. However, Aph. 66 of the *Centiloquy* attributed to Hermes contains the increase/decrease portion of the statement.

Chapt. 4. *How Much the Stars Add or Subtract to the Years of the Alcochoden.*

Years which the individual planets, when they are Alcochoden, denote in:

	Angles Greater	Succedents Medium	Cadents Lesser
Saturn	57	43 1/2	30
Jupiter	79	45 1/2	12
Mars	66	40 1/2	15
Sun	120	69 1/2	19
Venus	82	45	8
Mercury	76	48	20
Moon	108	66 1/2	25

When, therefore, you have recognized the quantity of years, months, and days the Alcochoden signified, and you want to know what the planets have added to or taken away from that amount, do this: consider carefully whether there is a fortune conjoined to it or aspecting it by trine or sextile aspect, [for] it will add to it its own lesser years; and if it is medium in its strength, so many months; and if it is weaker, days or hours. But if an evil [star] is joined to it or aspects it by square or opposite aspect, it will take away from it its minor years. And it must be known that the square and opposite rays of the fortunes add nothing to and subtract nothing from the Alcochoden, just as the sextiles and trines of the infortunes make neither an addition nor a diminution. Mercury, however, when it is with the fortunes (which add) will add his lesser years to it, and if it is with the evil [stars] will take them away. And of all [the stars], the one that impedites the Alcochoden the most is Mars. But when you know how many years the Alcochoden has given, direct the Hyleg with the degrees of ascension up to the point where it comes to the bodies or the rays of the evil [stars]. For when it comes to that point, it signifies the destruction of the native, without denying the omnipotence of God.

Chapt. 5. *The Native's Quality of Mind.*

When you want to know the habits of mind of the native, look at the lord of the ASC and at Mercury, which is the significator of the power of understanding, of language, and of speech. If it is in mobile signs, it signifies loftiness of intellect, catching on easily, excellence in and love of the different branches of knowledge, and religion. But if it is in common signs, it signifies a small intellect with a great quickness and speed to anger, and scanty and little stability and perseverance in undertakings or counsel or business. Finally, if it is in fixed signs, it signifies prudence, constancy, sympathy, and the completion of things undertaken.

But if both significators of the mind, viz. the lord of the ASC and Mercury, are oriental in an angle or a succedent of an angle, they signify goodness of mind and habits, and stability in doing things. But if you find them occidental and cadent, they signify ill temper and impudence of mind, and great gluttony, greediness, and quickness. And these signify things of the mind, just as the Moon and the ASC signify the body.

Besides this, whichever one of the planets is allotted the rulership of the chart has its own definite and separate significations over the things of the mind, which, insofar as it can be done (with God's assistance), we shall explain briefly and in order.

The Sun obtaining the rulership of the ASC, in a good house free [from any aspect of] the malefics, signifies depth of intellect, ease and adroitness of natural ability, and fear of God, and stability, first place, and rulership. But if it is impedited or cadent, it signifies commonness of mind, a man of no value, poor judgment, little knowledge, and many follies.

When the Moon is ruler of the ASC, in a suitable and favorable house in the circle, free from [any aspect of] the evil [stars], it signifies the growth of the native, beauty of face, and ease and completion of rearing and begetting. But if it is in an evil house, it signifies difficulty in rearing, a bad mind, hideousness of flesh, a stupid-looking face, and a poorly put-together body.

When Saturn is lord of the ASC and is in a good house, free from [any aspect of] the evil [stars], it signifies a man of great value, depth and singularity of counsel, and few questions. But if it is impedited in an evil house, it signifies a servile person, and one with ability of little value, ignobility of mind, and deceitful.

Jupiter lord of the ASC, in a good house free from [any aspect of] the evil [stars], promises first place, and nobility, and loftiness of mind. But if it is impedited in an evil house, it signifies whisperer, a hypocrite, and a liar.

Next, Mars lord of the ASC, free from [any aspect of] the evil [stars] in a suitable house, denotes boldness and rashness, rulership and leadership, excercise and renown in the lands and houses of kings. But when this same [planet] is impedited by the evil [stars] in an evil house, timidity and commonness of mind is signified, bad suspicion, and much entanglement in deeds and words.

Truly, when Venus occupies the rulership of the ASC posited in good house and free from [any aspect of] the evil [stars], it signifies a well put-together body, beauty, grace, and womanly characteristics, and joy. But if it is impedited in an evil house, it signifies nastiness, cunning, effeminacy,[18] prostituted virtue and modesty, and the shamelessness of sexual license.

---

18. The text has *mulierositatem* which usually means 'fondness for women', but in the last paragraph of this chapter it is paired with *virilitatis* 'virility', so I have translated it here 'effeminacy'.

But if Mercury is the lord of the ASC in a good house, free from [any aspect of] the infortunes, it bestows on the native eloquence, wisdom, grace, beauty, writing skill, knowledge, excellence and skill in invention and composition. If the same [planet] is impedited and in an evil house, the native will be deceitful, a liar, inclined to evil arts, and every sort of wickedness, a corrupter of letters,[19] and if there are any of this kind, [they are] liable to deceptions and frauds.[20]

Moreover, it is worth while to observe its application with the rest of the planets because it readily joins together with them. For if it is with Saturn or applies to it, it signifies seriousness of language, with acuity of intellect and much silence, investigation into medicine, and [a person] of careful opinions, but with the added nastiness of sexual license and lust.

The same [planet], if it is with Jupiter or applies to it, signifies honesty and prudence, acuteness, learning, and first place.

And if it is with Mars or applying to it, it signifies a constant gush of words, untruth and falsity, deception. If [the native] is masculine, he will be fond of women; if a woman, a virago.

But where it is found with the Sun or applies to it, the native will mingle with and attach himself to kings, princes and learned men.

And conjoined with Venus, either corporally or by rays, it signifies love of knowledge, counsel in lawsuits, and controversy among sects.

Lastly, when it is with the Moon or applies to her,[21] it signifies the love of change from one place to another, and much travel, with good consideration of things, and a love for all branches of knowledge.

Truly, this investigation of manliness or effeminacy,[22] strength or weakness, increase or decrease, in the qualities of mind of the native depends especially on the natures and qualities of the signs, viz. on the sex, strength, weakness, [and] increase of the signs in which the aforesaid significators of the mind are found. And this is the knowledge of the description of the mind and character of the native.

And now I shall make plain to you with this book of prognostics the doctrine of judgments, along with testimonies, that signify the nativities of kings.

---

19. Probably some sort of forger is meant.
20. The last two clauses are not clear. As they stand, they seem to refer to the "letters" that the native corrupts. Perhaps something has dropped out of the text.
21. Technically, the Moon would apply to Mercury.
22. In the text, the word *virilitatis* 'virility' is contrasted to *mulierositatis* which ought to mean 'fondness for women' but must mean 'effeminacy' here.

Chapt. 6. *Testimonies Signifying the Nativities of Kings.*

Look first at the degree of the ASC, for if there is in it any one
of the bright fixed stars of the first or second magnitude of the
nature of the good planets, or there is [one of them] joined to the
MC degree or to either of the luminaries, and especially to the Sun
in diurnal nativities or to the Moon in nocturnal nativities, or if
they are joined to two or three of these places, and the native is of
the race of kings or deserves to have kingship, it signifies the
noblest kind of kingship.[23] And if he is not worthy of kingship, his
commands will be carried out just like the commands of a king. But he
will be under the hands of a king, and he will be put in charge of
the management of embassies, [and] in charge of the people, doing
good or evil to them, and he will attain elevation and very great
power.

But if the Sun is in its own exaltation in diurnal nativities, or
the Moon is in its own exaltation in nocturnal nativities, or in the
MC, or in the ASC, or rising, or the ASC is a royal sign, and the
lord of the ASC is in the same house, or it is in the MC, it
signifies the nativities of kings if the native is of the royal stock
or of one which is worthy of a kingdom, or he will attain to a
dignity like that of a king in which he will manage public affairs.

And when the Sun in diurnal nativities, or the Moon in nocturnal
nativities, is in the degree of its own exaltation, it signifies
kingship. Also, those luminaries applying to the lord of the ASC, if
it is in its own exaltation, oriental, in any angle, signify the
nativities of kings, or of such persons as attain to royal dignity.
And if the lord of the MC applies to the lord of the ASC and both are
in angles, oriental, and in their own exaltations, they denote that
the native will have either royal dignity and power, or involvement
with it, or something similar in which he has the management of
public affairs.

Similarly, when all the planets are applying to Jupiter, and it is
in the MC, oriental, in its own exaltation, it signifies kingship. In
the same exact manner, other planets too, when they are in the MC,
oriental, in their own exaltations, will signify kingship. And the
Sun, when it is received in the MC, and the Moon is in trine aspect
to it, will signify rulership.

The same thing is denoted by the lord of the triplicity of the ASC
when it applies to the lord of the ASC, or when the lord of the ASC
is in the MC, or oriental in the ASC. Also, you will consider the
dustoria[24] of the planets that are diurnal with respect to the Sun
and nocturnal with respect to the Moon, [i.e.] when they are oriental
to the Sun and occidental to the Moon, and in their own exaltations
or domiciles, and the luminaries are in their own exaltations or

---

23. Here, the author makes an important point: the native's circumstances of birth must be taken
into account before rendering a judgment. Cf. William Lilly, *Christian Astrology*, pp. 616-7, who
expands on the same theme.
    24. An Arabic term from the Middle Persian for a planet which is in a position of power to the
right of the Sun and past combustion. Abu 'Ali also applies it by analogy to the position of
planets with respect to the Moon.

their own domiciles, in angles mutually aspecting each other, they signify kings or those like unto them.

Chapt. 7 *The Native's Prosperity and Adversity.*

With regard to the matter of the native's prosperity[25] and property,[26] and whether he will attain to much or little of it, look at the lords of the triplicity of that luminary which has the rulership of the time.[27] Because if they are in angles free from [the aspects of] the malefic stars and from impediments, they signify that the native will be prosperous all the days of his life. And especially if the first lord[28] of the triplicity is in the first fifteen degrees of its sign,[29] because then the native will prosper more. And the closer it is to the degree of any angle, the better it will be and the greater the prosperity of the native. But if it is in the other degrees of the angle after the aforesaid 15, he will not prosper so much as I said above, but just to a lomited degree, and [likewise] if the planet is in a succedent [house]. Also, with the first lord of the triplicity placed fortunately as I have said, if the second and third [lords] are cadent and impedited, the first lord of the triplicity signifies the prosperity of the native in the beginning of his life, and the others signify adversity and harm in the middle and in the end of the native's life.

In the same fashion, if the first lord of the triplicity is cadent and impedited by the evil [stars], but the remaining two [lords] are in angles, free from impediments and [the aspects of] the evil [stars], the first lord of the triplicity signifies that the native will have adversity and misfortune in the beginning of life; but he will be prosperous in the middle and the end of life. But when all the lords of the triplicity, the lords of the *Anauba*,[30] are cadent and impedited, they signify that the native will have hard work and adversity and shortness of life. Still, with these so placed, if fortunes are in the angles and the evil [stars] are cadent, prosperity is signified for the native. And if the luminaries are in a good state, they signify happiness and the reward of high position for the native. Furthermore, if the lord of the ASC and the Moon are in angles free from [the aspects of] the evil [stars] and from impediments, and she applies to planets in angles, they promise prosperity for the native, especially if they are received.

---

25. The word 'prosperity' encompasses the native's good fortune in all aspects of life, not just in financial matters.

26. The word 'property' refers to all the native's possessions.

27. The so-called 'Lord of the Time', i.e. the Sun in a diurnal nativity, and the Moon in a nocturnal nativity.

28. Each triplicity has three rulers. The first two reverse at night. By 'first lord' Abu 'Ali means the one that is named first in sequence for the time of day when the birth took place.

29. He means 'house'. Cf. what follows.

30. That is, the 'lords of the time' from the Arabic *al-nawba* 'turn' or 'time', referring to a particular space of time. Here, the lords of the triplicity, each of which rules a particular space of time.

And if the lord of the ASC applies to the luminaries, and they are
found to be in their exaltations or their domiciles, or if the
luminaries apply to the lord of the ASC and it is in its exaltation
or in its own domicile, they signify good fortune for the native
throughout his whole life.

But if the Part of Fortune and its lord are free from [the aspects
of] the evil [stars] and oriental [planets] aspect the ASC from
angles, they signify lasting good fortune for the native and
greatness of his worth and reputation. But if these same
significators are cadent and impedited, they threaten the native with
hard work and little prosperity, and especially if they do not aspect
the ASC.

When the lords of the ASC are cadent from the angles, but applying
to planets in angles, they signify prosperity after hard work.
Similarly, when the lord of the ASC is cadent and in its fall, and it
applies to a planet that is in its own domicile or exaltation, it
signifies prosperity that will follow after hard work. And the
[horoscopes that follow] are in fact similar to those that the
ancients proved by experience in their significations of prosperity
and hard work.[31]

---

31. The horoscopes that follow also appear at the end of the short text on nativities by
Masha'allah edited by Pingree (E.S. Kennedy and David Pingree *The Astrological History of
Masha'allah*, Appendix 3). Pingree has identified three of them as coming from Dorotheus, one from
Rhetorius, and the others perhaps from a sixth century Greek compilation. He has also determined
tentative dates for the horoscopes. No places or dates are given in the texts or sources (with one
exception), nor have any of the horoscopes been identified as those of historical personages. The
charts are given in square form in both Pingree's book and the printed edition of Abu 'Ali (which
has charts for only the first four). I have drawn them in the round form, since the square form is
obsolete. Several of them have internal inconsistencies. See Appendix 1 for further details.

[1.] A Nocturnal Nativity with Gemini Ascending.

The Sun and Venus in Leo,   Saturn and the Moon in Scorpio, Mars in
Aquarius,   Jupiter in Taurus,   and   Mercury in Virgo signify in this
figure the bad luck of this native from the lords of the triplicity
of the Moon because the nativity was nocturnal. And the first lord of
this triplicity was Mars, the   second Venus, both cadent from the
angles, which signified poverty and bad conditions for the native.
And therefore this native was a pauper, and he only got his food by
hard work.

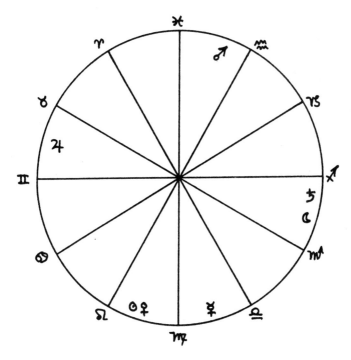

[2/3 Aug 43]

[From Dorotheus's *Pentateuch*.]

[2.] A Diurnal[32] Nativity with Aries Ascending.

The Sun and Mercury in Aquarius, the Moon in Sagittarius, Saturn and Mars in Scorpio, Jupiter in Cancer, and Venus in Capricorn. The luck of this native is signified by the lords of the triplicity of the Sun because the nativity was diurnal. The first lord of this triplicity was Saturn, the second Mercury, both in [houses] succedent to the angles. Saturn in fact was in the succedent to the angle of the occident and Mercury in the succedent to the MC angle, which [together] signified prosperity and wealth and much property. This native, therefore, had extensive possessions, was abounding in money [and enjoyed] the highest honor and the greatest prosperity.

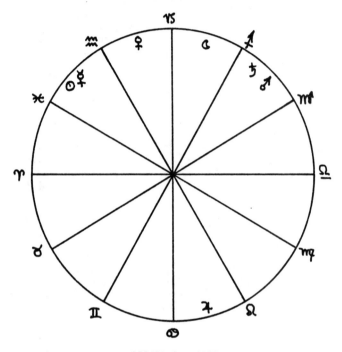

[29/30 Jan 425]

[See Appendix 1.]

---

32. The printed Latin text has 'Nocturnal' in error.

[3.] A Nocturnal Nativity with Scorpio Ascending.

The Moon in Scorpio, the Sun in Aries, Mars in Aquarius, Venus in Taurus, Mercury in Pisces, Jupiter and Saturn in Virgo. The luck of this native is signified by the lords of the triplicity of the Moon because the nativity was nocturnal. The first lord of the triplicity of the Moon was Mars, the second Venus, the third the Moon, all in angles, which signified prosperity, lofty position, and kingship. And consequently this man was great, of high degree, and steady in prosperity until a golden crown was placed upon his head, and a silver one with pearls and precious stones, and his praise was in the mouths of all men.

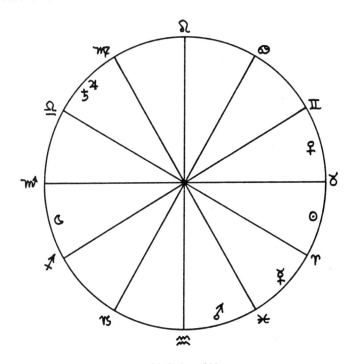

[1/2 Apr 36]

[From Dorotheus's *Pentateuch*]

[4.] A Diurnal Nativity with Cancer Ascending.

The Sun and Mercury in Aries, Jupiter and the Moon in Cancer, Saturn in Pisces, Venus in Virgo, and Mars in Scorpio. This figure signifies the luck of the native from the lords of the triplicity of the Sun because the nativity was diurnal. And the first lord of this triplicity was the Sun, the second Jupiter, both in angles and in their own exaltations, which signified his lofty position and good fortune, and ample means, good reputation, and the greatest praise among kings and nobles. And Saturn, the third lord of the triplicity, did not impedite him although it was cadent from an angle in a domicile of Jupiter and they aspected each other by trine aspect; therefore they signified that this native was honored and highly praised among the highest kings.

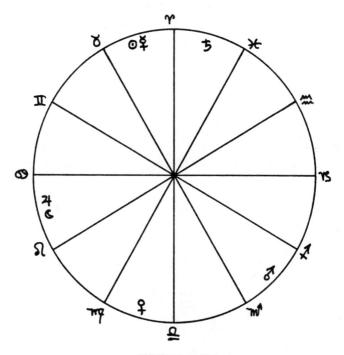

[29/30 Mar 22]

[From Dorotheus's *Pentateuch*.]

[5.] A Nocturnal Nativity with Cancer Ascending.

Jupiter and the Moon in Gemini, Saturn, the Sun, and Mercury in Scorpio, Mars and Venus in Leo. The luck of this native is signified by the lords of the triplicity of the Moon because the nativity was nocturnal. The first lord of this triplicity was Mercury and the second Saturn, cadent from the angles, the signification of which portended want and poverty. But Jupiter, the third lord of this triplicity, was in the [house] succedent to the angle of the MC, which moderated and restrained the bad luck arising from the other two just mentioned.[33] Therefore, this native had a moderate life, such as that led by religious persons.

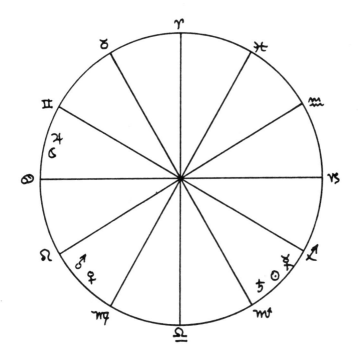

[See Appendix 1.]

---

33. As can be seen from the chart, the positions specified in the text do not agree with the commentary. Something is wrong. See Appendix 1 for a discussion of the problem. In the meantime, imagine a chart with Mercury and Saturn in the 3rd, 6th, 9th, or 12th house and Jupiter in the 11th. Such a chart indicates a moderate life because the good position of Jupiter acts to offset the evil arising from the cadency of Mercury and Saturn. This is the point Abu 'Ali wished to make with this chart.

[6.] A Diurnal Nativity with Gemini Ascending.

The Sun, Saturn, and the Moon in Pisces, Mercury and Jupiter in Aries, Mars in Virgo, and Venus in Taurus. I considered the luck of this native from the lords of the triplicity of the Sun because the nativity was diurnal. The first lord of it was the Sun, the second Jupiter, and the third Saturn, all being in angles,[34] the signification of which suggested good fortune and much wealth; and therefore this man was of high position and rich, having much gold and silver.

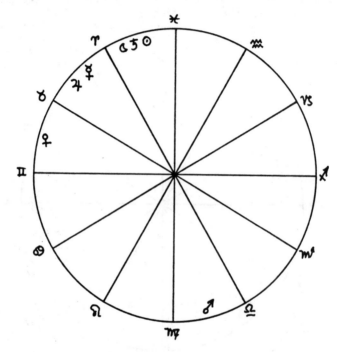

[24/25 Mar 434?]

[See Appendix 1.]

---

34. Here again the planetary positions given do not agree with the commentary. Masha'allah's chart puts the Sun in Aries, and this is probably correct because the commentary assumes the Sun is in a Fire sign. However, doing so puts the Sun in the 11th house. See Appendix 1 for further comment. Abu 'Ali wanted to give an example of a chart with all three triplicity rulers angular.

[7.] A Diurnal Nativity with the Beginning of Scorpio Ascending.

Jupiter in the 21st degree and 12th minute of Libra, the Sun in
the 8th of Libra, Mercury in the 11th degree and 15th minute of
Scorpio, Saturn in the 15th degree of Taurus, the Moon in the 26th
degree of Leo, Mars in the 18th degree of Virgo, the Part of Fortune
in the 18th degree of Virgo, [Venus in the 28th degree of Virgo],[35]
and the Head of the Dragon of the Moon in the 8th degree and 40th
minute of Taurus. This configuration signifies the luck of this
native from the lords of the triplicity of the Sun because the
nativity was diurnal. The first lord of it was Saturn, the second
Mercury, and the third Jupiter. Each of which was harmful to another.
For Saturn was in opposition to Mercury and conjunct the Head of the
Dragon and cadent,[36] Jupiter similarly cadent, and the Part of
Fortune with Mars, and the lord of the Part conjoined to the Tail in
opposition to Saturn, which signified hard work and few good things,
and mental confusion, which so happened to this native.

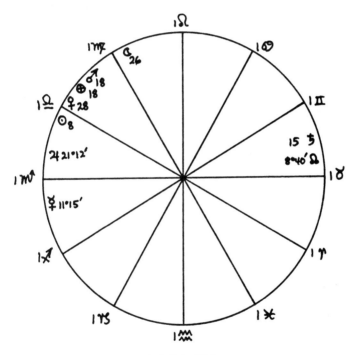

[19 Oct 439]

[See Appendix 1.]

---

35. I have restored this position from Masha'allah's chart.
36. Saturn is not cadent. Masha'allah's commentary reads 'and Mercury conjunct Cauda, and Saturn
with Caput, and Jupiter cadent', which is preferable to the reading in Abu 'Ali's text.

[8.] A Nocturnal Nativity with Virgo Ascending.

The Moon in Gemini, Saturn, the Sun, and Mercury in Aquarius, Mars in Capricorn,[37] Venus in Sagittarius, and Jupiter in Virgo. The luck of this native is signified by the lords of the triplicity of the Moon, for it was a nocturnal birth. And the first lord of the triplicity was Mercury, the second Saturn, both cadent, which signified poverty and a bad condition for this native, and so in fact it happened that this man was of narrow means, abounding in nothing other than sweat and hard work. But because Jupiter and Venus were in angles, they signified bodily health and good rearing, and sustenance from kings and princes and from many friends.

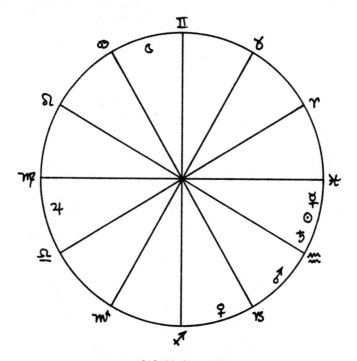

[19/20 Jan 403]

[See Appendix 1.]

---

37. It is actually in Aquarius.

[9.] A Nocturnal Nativity with the 16th Degree of Gemini Ascending.

The Moon in the 16th degree of Aries, Jupiter in the 22nd of
Scorpio, Venus in the 13th degree of Scorpio, Saturn in the 15th
degree of Pisces, Mercury in the 21st of Scorpio,[38] the Sun in the
9th degree of Sagittarius, Mars in the 19th of Sagittarius, the Head
of the Dragon in the 23rd degree of Capricorn, and the Part of
Fortune in the 9th degree of Aquarius. The luck of this native was
signified by the lords of the triplicity of the Moon because the
nativity was nocturnal. The first lord of it was Jupiter, the second
the Sun, both cadent from the angles in the sixth sign, which
suggested the signification of hard work for the native and few good
things. Then I looked at the Part of Fortune, and I found it in the
ninth sign,[39] and its lord not aspecting it, which also signified
hard work and want.

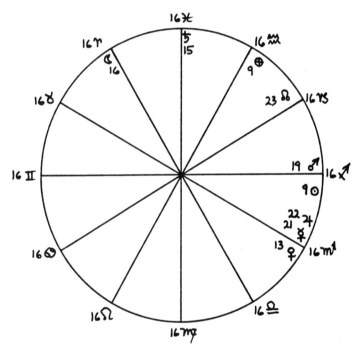

[25 Nov 464]

[See Appendix 1.]

---

38. Mercury is actually in 21 Sagittarius. This same error is found in Masha'allah's chart.
Astrologically, the position in Sagittarius is worse than the one in Scorpio, for although it is
angular, Mercury is in its detriment in Sagittarius, it is conjunct the malefic Mars, and square
the malefic Saturn.
39. In the 9th sign, but not in the 9th house of the Equal House system.

[10.] A Nocturnal Nativity with the Twenty-first Degree of Taurus
Ascending.

The Moon in the first degree of Pisces, the Sun in the 17th degree
of Virgo, Saturn in the 14th degree of Sagittarius, Jupiter in the
17th degree of Libra, Mars in the 21st degree of Virgo, Venus in the
17th degree of Leo, Mercury in the 5th degree of Libra, the Part of
Fortune in the 7th of Sagittarius, and the Head of the Dragon in the
8th degree of Capricorn. The luck of this native is signified by the
lords of the triplicity of the Moon because the nativity was
nocturnal. The first lord of it was Mars, under the Sun beams in
square aspect to Saturn, which signified hard work and anxiety for
the native in the first third of his life. But the second lord of the
triplicity was Venus, and it was lord of the ASC in an angle, and
increasing in its number,⁴⁰ signifying prosperity and good conditions
for the native after hard work. Also, Jupiter and Mercury, which are
in the sixth sign descending towards the fifth, denote [hard work and
little good. But they are also in the 11th house] from the Part of
Fortune,⁴¹ [which signifies] prosperity and good position for the
native.⁴² And so it happened to the native.

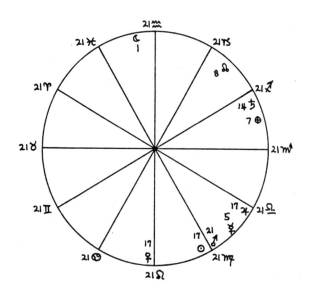

[8 Sep 428 9:15 P.M. LMT]

[From Rhetorius. See Appendix 1.]

---

40. That is, it is direct in motion. According to the Equal House system it is cadent, but it is
in the 4th sign of the Sign-House system, hence angular.
41. Reading a *parte fortunae* from the Part of Fortune' instead of *apertae fortunae* 'open
fortune'.
42. Cf. Chapt. 11, where a fortune in the 11th from the Part of Fortune is said to produce this
effect.

[11.] A Nocturnal Nativity with the 2nd Degree and 30th Minute of
Libra Ascending.

ASC in the 2nd degree and 30th minute of Libra, the Moon in the
8th degree and 4th minute of Cancer, Saturn in the 2nd degree of
Gemini, Jupiter in the 15th degree of Sagittarius, the Sun in the
10th degree of Aquarius, Mars in the 15th degree of Sagittarius,
Venus in the 25th degree of Pisces, Mercury in the 15th degree of
Aquarius, and the Part of Fortune in the 10th degree of Taurus. This
chart signifies the luck of this native from the lords of the
triplicity of the Moon, for the nativity was nocturnal. The first
lord of it was Mars, the second Venus, both cadent in the sixth and
the third, which signified bad circumstances for the native. But the
Moon, which was the luminary of the time, was in the MC, she also
being the last lord of the triplicity; and the Part of Fortune, was
of the nature of Venus; [together they] signified beauty and good
circumstances for the native at the end of his life.

For whenever the lords of the triplicity of the luminary which has
the rulership are cadent, look at the Part of Fortune because it
signifies great and lofty things when it is conjoined to Jupiter or
to Venus or is applying to them by aspect.

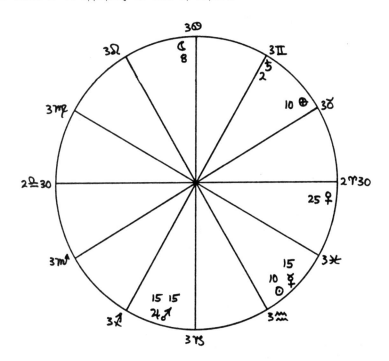

[7 Feb 442]

[See Appendix 1.]

[12.] A Diurnal Nativity with the 10th Degree and 7th Minute of
Cancer Ascending.

The Sun in the 24th [degree] of Aries, the Moon in the 17th of
Libra, Saturn in the 27th of Libra, Jupiter in the 17th of
Sagittarius, Mars in Sagittarius, the Part of Fortune in the 18th of
Sagittarius,[43] and the Head [of the Dragon] in the 17th of Scorpio.
The luck of this native was signified by the lords of the triplicity
of the Sun, for the nativity was diurnal. And the Sun was the first
lord of the triplicity, in his own exaltation in the MC, applied to
Saturn but not received by it, and Jupiter the second lord, and the
lord of the MC were cadent in the sixth sign. And Saturn, the third
lord, in his own exaltation, signified prosperity for the native in
the end of his life. I looked again further at the Part of Fortune,
and I found it in the sixth sign conjoined to Jupiter, and the Moon
in the MC of the Part of Fortune, which signified good fortune from
middle life down to the end of it.

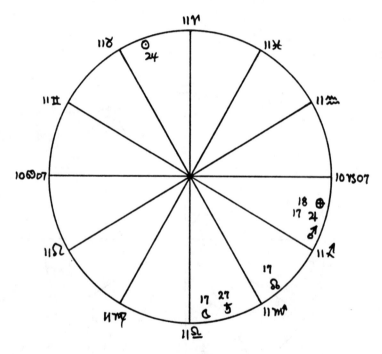

[3 Apr 394?]

[See Appendix 1.]

---

43. This position of the Part of Fortune is inconsistent with the positions of the Sun, the
Moon, and the ASC degree. Perhaps the Moon should be in Virgo.

And so much for examples. Now we shall return to the rules themselves.

When the lord of the triplicity of that luminary which has the dignity is impeded, look at the Part of Fortune. If it is in an angle and fortunes and infortunes alike aspect it, it signifies middling circumstances and prosperity. Also, look at the lords of the triplicity of the Sun in diurnal nativities and the lords of the triplicity of the Moon at night. If they are in angles, they signify greatness and excellent circumstances. But if they are cadent, they signify hard work and a bad existence. But if either of the evil [planets] is in the 11th sign from the ASC, or with the Part of Fortune, or with the Sun in diurnal nativities, or with the Moon in nocturnal nativities, it signifies the loss of good fortune, and especially if it does not have any dignity in the sign. And if the Part of Fortune or its lord does not aspect the ASC or the Sun in diurnal nativities or the Moon in nocturnal nativities, it signifies the loss of good fortune, and especially if it does not have any dignity in the sign.

And in fact the Moon, in nocturnal nativities, signifies the loss of good fortune in this way: if the Moon is separated from evil [planets] and its next application is to evil [planets], it signifies the loss of good fortune; and if the Alcochoden is in an evil house and the evil [planets] aspect it, it signifies the loss of good fortune. Besides this, if evil [planets] are in the angles and fortunes in the succedents of the angles, it signifies hard work in the beginning of life and good fortune in the end of it. And if the Sun in day nativities and the Moon in night nativities is separated from evil [planets] and applies to good [planets], it signifies a good existence for the native and his rise after hard work. And if the lords of the lunar triplicity (when it has the dignity) are cadent, applying to planets that are in their own exaltations or domiciles, it signifies good fortune for the native after hard work. And when the luminaries are impeded, without any aspect to the fortunes, it signifies a good existence for the native after hard work.

Chapt. 8. *The Time of the Native's Good Fortune.*

Know that if the planet that signifies good fortune is oriental above the earth, it signifies good fortune in the beginning of life; and if it is occidental below the earth, it signifies good fortune in the end of life. Furthermore, you will also consider the application of the houses, because the rising sign and the 2nd [sign] signify the beginning of life and adolescence, the 10th and the 11th signify youth, the 7th and the 8th old age, the 4th and the 5th the age of decrepitude and the end of life.

Also, the Part of Fortune signifies the beginning of life and its lord the end of it. And the one of them that is in the more favorable house and condition will signify the goodness of the native's existence in its own time.

Also, you will explore the time of prosperity or of misfortune or
of middling circumstances of the native more fully; namely, from the
direction of the planets, which will signify this thing by the
distance that is between them and the fortunes or the evil [planets]
in signs, degrees, and minutes. In addition, you will direct the Part
of Fortune to the bodies of the fortunate as well as the malefic
stars and to the rays of these same. Because, when it is conjunct or
applied to Jupiter or to Venus, it signifies good fortune in that
time; and when it is conjunct or it applies to Saturn or to Mars, it
signifies the loss of the native's money and the depopulation of his
home.

Chapt. 9. *The Sources of the Native's Prosperity.*

Look at the source of prosperity and property, viz. the Part of
Fortune.[44] And if it is in the exaltation of the Sun, [the native]
will be rendered fortunate by association with kings and princes. And
if it is in the exaltation of Jupiter, his fortune will come from
connection with nobles and great men and religious persons. But if it
is in the exaltation of Mars, his fortune will come from connection
with military commanders and warlike men. But if it is in the
exaltation of Venus, his fortune will come from friendship with women
and effeminate men.

But if it is in the exaltation of Mercury, his fortune will come
from learned men, scribes, and wise men. But if it is in the
exaltation of the Moon, his fortune will come from association with
slaves, the public, and legal witnesses.

Finally, if it is in the exaltation of Saturn, fortune will come
to the native from association with slaves and slave-girls on farms,
and old men. Further, in like manner, you will judge from the term
and the domicile where the Part of Fortune is, and especially if its
lord aspects it.

When the Part of Fortune is in an angle it signifies great good
fortune, but in a cadent [house] hard work and difficulty in
acquiring things.

And in addition, the place of the Moon in the circle and her
configuration with the planets must be known, for it has a strong
signification from the planet to which it is joined.[45] When it is in
the domicile of Venus, conjoined or applying to it, it signifies that
the native will be fond of joy, play, and delight. And if iy is in
the domicile of Jupiter, either aspecting it or with it, it signifies
that the native will be magnanimous, and he will have friendship with
kings, and he will be religious and fortunate, famous and praised by
all. And if it is in the domicile of Mars, joined or applying to it,
it signifies that the native will be bold and a lover of brawling and
warfare; and he will be a man involved in hard work and traveling,

----

44. The printed text has *apertae fortunae* 'open fortune' in error for *partis fortunae* 'Part of
Fortune'. This same misreading occurs in example Chart 10 in Chapt. 7 above.
45. In the printed text this sentence is erroneously included in the same paragraph with the
preceding sentence about the Part of Fortune.

with much endurance, and he will associate with warlike men and be
fortunate through them. And if it is in the domicile of Mercury,
configured with it either corporally or by rays, it signifies that
the native will be shrewd, ingenious, wise, skilled in the law of
inheritances and in disputes; and he will attain a fortune and
benefit through these things. But if it is in the domicile of Saturn,
conjoined or applying to it, he will be of a cold nature, sad, having
much hard work and anxiety in acquiring food and resources unless
Saturn is oriental, for then inheritances, resources, and many new
buildings will come to him in abundance.

But if it is in the domicile of the Sun, conjoined to it, it
signifies that the native will have scanty property and a short life
and much infirmity. But when it applies to the Sun by trine or
sextile aspect, it signifies that the native will gain benefit from
highly-placed men, or he will be one of their number, and [in either
case] well-off. And I say the same about the lord of the exaltation
and the [lord of] the term as I said about the lord of the domicile.

Chapt. 10. *The Native's Circumstances, and the Things Signified by the First House.*

Look at the lords of the triplicity of the ASC because the first
lord of this triplicity signifies the beginning of life, the second
the middle, and the third the end. But if one of them is in its own
domicile or exaltation, in an angle or a succedent of an angle,
applying to the fortunes and free from [any aspect of] the evil
[planets], it signifies good circumstances for the native in its own
time of his life.

And if one of them is in an evil house, combust, retrograde, or in
its fall, or applied to evil [planets], it signifies bad conditions
for the native in its own time of his life. And consider the aspects
of the lord of the triplicity, first to the lord of the ASC, second
to the lord of the MC, and third to the lord of the 7th house,
because if both[46] are well placed, it will be a greater signification
for good; and if both are impedited, it will be a greater
signification for evil.

Next look at the Moon's application to the planets in the hour of
the nativity to apprehend the native's circumstances. And if it is
[also] separated from [some of] the planets, the native's condition
is divided into two modes, of which one will be dependent upon the
Moon's sign and its place in the houses of the circle, and the second
upon the lord of the Moon's house and its house and the place of it
from the Sun,[47] and its application to the planets, and, conversely,
their application to it.

---

46. He seems to mean "the lord of the triplicity and the lord of any one of the three houses named."

47. Exactly what he means by "place of it from the Sun" is not clear. Most likely he refers to orientality and avoidance of combustion. Cf. the same phrase in the first paragraph of the next chapter.

Look further at the lord of the ASC and its place in the houses of
the circle. Because if it is in the ASC, it signifies that the native
will be honored among his near relations and servants and
acquaintances. If it is in the 2nd from the ASC, he will be the
destroyer of his own estate. But if it is received there, he will
profit and make gains. But in the 3rd house of heaven from the ASC,
it signifies that he will have suitable brothers and will travel
much. In the 4th, that he will be good spirited and will attain very
great benefits from his parents. In the 5th, that he will rejoice
with children, and he will have many friends. In the 6th, that he
will be harassed by very great and numerous labors and infirmities.
In the 7th, that he will be quarrelsome, easily angered, and one who
follows the wishes of women. In the 8th, that he will be deceitful,
with much sadness, and weak-spirited. In the 9th, that he will travel
much and will be a lover of knowledge. In the 10th, that he will
always be with kings and will get his living from them. In the 11th,
that he will be endowed with good character and will have many
friends but few children. In the 12th, that he will lead a bad life
and have many enemies.

Chapt. 11. *The Native's Wealth*[48] *and its Sources, and the Things Signified by the Second House.*

Look at the second house from the ASC, because if fortunes are in
it or aspect it, and the evil [planets] are not in it and do not
aspect it, and its lord is in a good place in the circle and from the
Sun, it will signify good fortune and success for the native in
acquiring assets. But if these same dispose themselves in contrary
fashion, it portends loss for the native in portions of his wealth.
Then look too at the lord of the 2nd sign. If it applies to the lord
of the ASC, it signifies the acquisition of much money without any
hard work. But if conversely the lord of the ASC applies to the lord
of the 2nd house, it signifies an increase in assets to be sure, but
with hard work.

After this, consider whether this application is made from an
angle. And if it happens so, it signifies much wealth [arising] from
things already known. But if the application is from a succedent of
an angle, it certainly takes away something from the abovesaid
happiness and ease [of acquisition] of good fortune. But nevertheless
the native will be good-spirited. Aside from this, if the application
is from an evil house and one not aspecting the ASC, it signifies a
motley acquisition for the native, neither good nor bad, that is, he
won't care whether he acquires from a good [source] or from a bad
[one] with avarice and servility.

Moreover, if there is no application between the lord of the ASC
and the 2nd sign, then look at the lord of the 2nd. If it is in an
angle, free from [any aspect with] the evil [planets], and the Moon
[is posited] similarly, the native will have a moderate living. But
if it is cadent, he will encounter difficulties in the acquisition of

---

48. I use the word 'wealth' to translate the Latin *substantia*, which means something like 'total
assets'. It includes money, personal possessions, real estate, and everything else of value. It
carries no implication of size—it simply means 'whatever assets there are'.

necessities, and especially if it is also impedited by the evil
[planets].

Following this, consider too the lord of the ASC and Jupiter. If
one applies to the other, it signifies prosperity and ample means,
especially if reception also accompanies the application. Similarly
too, if the Part [of Fortune?] and its lord are in good houses in the
circle, free from [any aspect of] the evil [planets], and aspecting
the ASC, it signifies riches and many good things.

Similarly, if the Moon is received while aspecting the ASC, it
signifies that the native will have riches and good circumstances,
but especially if the star that receives is a fortune. The same when
she is in an angle or the succedent of an angle, increased in light
and in number,[49] and the planets which receive her have conjoined
their own disposition and virtue, it signifies an influx of benefits
to the native and a great good fortune and a succession of things
coming to him incessantly.

Consider also the lords of the triplicity of the 2nd house because
they also have signification in matters of wealth in accordance with
their own nature and strength. And if the first of these is free from
[any aspect of] the evil [planets], [the native] will have good
[circumstances] in the beginning of his life. And if the second
[lord] is strong, he will attain that in the middle of his life. And
if the third is likewise strong, good things will happen to him in
the end of his life.

Furthermore, if any one of the fortunes is in the 11th sign from
the Part of Fortune, it signifies the acquisition of money and of
assets from good things.[50] But if any one of the evil [planets] is in
the 11th sign from the Part of Fortune, it signifies that the native
will use fraud and injustice in the acquisition of money, and
especially if it is in its own domicile or exaltation. And when the
lord of the house of wealth[51] and the lord of the Part of Fortune
become combust, it signifies evil circumstances for the native and a
diminution of his property.

When the Part of Fortune is conjunct the fortunes or is in square
or opposition aspect to them and the evil [planets] fall away[52] from
it, it signifies much benefit to the native and to his fortune. And
when it is conjunct the evil [planets] or is in square or opposite
aspect to them and the fortunes do not aspect it, it signifies evil
conditions for the native and little of anything good.

When the lord of the ASC and [the lord] of the 2nd sign do not
apply one to the other, and the fortunes fall away from the ASC and
the 2nd, it signifies hard work for the native and bad circumstances
all the days of his life. And still investigating the many
testimonies that signify assets, consider the application of the lord
of the ASC or the lord of the 2nd house, and the lords of the

---

49. The phrase "increased in number" means *direct* in motion.
50. Cf. example Chart 10 in Chapt. 7.
51. The 2nd house.
52. That is, they are not in aspect with it.

triplicity of that luminary which obtains the lordship of the time,
and [the lords] of the Part of Fortune and the Part of Wealth⁵³ and
[the dispositor] of Jupiter, because if you find one, or two, or
three of these planets that have several dignities and are free from
[any aspect of] the evil [planets] and are in good places in the
circle [of houses] and from the Sun, it signifies good circumstances
for the native in assets and fortune according to their place and
motion. But if the greater part of them are cadent or impedited, it
signifies bad prospects for the native in money matters in accordance
with the degree of their evil and their place in the circle.

    Furthermore, the places of the significator of wealth, or of the
lord of the 2nd, ought to be considered. For if the lord of the 2nd
sign is in the ASC, it signifies that the native will acquire money
without hard work and without anxiety; and if it is received there,
there will be the greatest good luck in good things, and especially
when it is received by a benefic and fortunate star placed in an
angle. If it is in the 2nd house, there will be acquisition, and his
livelihood will be from some known thing, and he will not heap up
money. If it is in the 3rd, it portends evil conditions for the
brothers and hard work for them. But in the 4th, good circumstances
for the parents and continuance of the native in that house in which
he was born, and excellence of his conditions. In the 5th, he will
have children who are known in the king's palace, and they will have
many good things. If it is in the 6th, it implies the flight of
slaves and the loss of animals, and he will be a spendthrift. But in
the 7th, it portends the accumulation of things through unjust means
and their dispersion on women and contracts. And if the lord of the
2nd sign is in the 8th, it signifies that the native will acquire
wealth from inheritances and from something to do with the dead; and
he will be a spendthrift, and he will not care how he spends or gains
[money]. And if it is in the 9th house of heaven, it signifies that
he will be an acquirer of wealth from travels and from something to
do with religion, and he will not care about anything except absent
things, and his business will have to do with travel and travelers.
And if it is in the 10th, he will attain wealth from the king and
from his affairs, and from that source he will get his living. If in
the 11th, he will find his wealth from friends and business agents
and negociators or from [handling] goods. Finally, if it is in the
12th, he will acquire resources and money from prisons and enemies
and from every [sort of] vile and shameful [kind of] work, and he
will be a thief and a robber.

---

53. Abu ʿAli assumes we know how to calculate the Part of Wealth. Dorotheus (*Pentateuch* i. 27)
gives us the formula: Cusp of the 2nd House – Lord of the 2nd + ASC. Al-Biruni (*The Book of
Instruction*, Sect. 476) gives the same formula for diurnal nativities, but Lord of the 2nd – Cusp
of the 2nd + ASC for nocturnal nativities. Ibn Ezra (*The Beginning of Wisdom*, Chapt. 9) agrees with
Dorotheus.

Chapt. 12 *The Fortune of the Brothers.*

Look at the third sign from the ASC and its lord, and which of the
fortunate or the evil planets are there, or which [planets] aspect it
by square or opposite aspect. Because if the fortunes are there or
they are in aspect, it signifies good fortune for the brothers and
much prosperity for them. But if the evil [planets] are there, or if
they aspect the house by square or opposite aspect, it signifies bad
conditions for the brothers and little good for them.

But if the third sign from the ASC is one of those signs
signifying many brothers and its lord is in a similar [sign], it
signifies many brothers. And if it is one of the signs signifying few
brothers and its lord is in a similar [sign], it signifies few
brothers. But the signs signifying many children are Cancer, Scorpio,
and Pisces; and [those signifying] few children are Leo, Virgo,
Capricorn, and Aquarius. And the rest of the signs are middling as to
few or many children.

And when the sign of brothers is common and its lord is in a
common sign, it signifies that he will have brothers from his father
only or from his mother. And if the lord of the sign of brothers is
going into combustion, it signifies few brothers. The separation of
the Moon from Saturn in an angle in a nocturnal nativity or from Mars
in a diurnal nativity, signifies the death of the elder brothers.

When the native's ASC is one of the signs signifying many
children, and the Moon is similarly placed, it signifies many
brothers and sisters from the mother only. And when the native's ASC
is the 3rd degree of Scorpio, it signifies that the native will not
have brothers or sisters from his own mother. Next, look at Mars and
its sign with regard to brothers. If it is in a sign of many children
and its lord is oriental, it signifies many brothers, and especially
if the ASC is Leo or Sagittarius and the Moon is in [one of] those
[signs].

When Mars enters into combustion, it signifies few brothers and
the death of the elder ones. And if there is a peregrine or an evil
planet in the third sign, it signifies few brothers. But if Mars and
the lord of its triplicity is in a suitable place in the circle [of
houses] and from the Sun, it signifies the agreement and strength of
the brothers and much benefit. And if it is in its own fall or its
own detriment or going into combustion or the lords of its triplicity
are in evil houses, it signifies few brothers and debility and bad
conditions for them. Besides all this, if the lords of the triplicity
of the ASC are cadent, it signifies few brothers. And if they are in
middling signs, it signifies that they will be mediocre. Look also at
the Part of Brothers[54] and its lord, because, if their testimonies
are the same, their effect will be stronger and their judgment more

---

54. Firmicus (*Mathesis* VI.xxxii.23) gives the formula: Jupiter - Saturn + ASC by day, and the
reverse by night. Dorotheus (*Pentateuch* i.19) has: Jupiter - Saturn + ASC by day, and ASC -
(Jupiter - Saturn) by night, which is of course equivalent to Saturn - Jupiter + ASC. But here we
see foreshadowed an error that will appear in the *Pentateuch* when we come to the Part of the
Father.

certain. But if they are different, the testimonies of the third sign
and its lord will be stronger.

Chapt. 13. *The Number of Brothers.*

Consider the lords of the triplicity of the ASC. If they are in
the ASC, the native will be his mother's first born. And if they are
in the MC, he will be the first or the tenth. If in the Angle of
Earth,[55] he will be the first or the fourth. If in the 7th, he will
be the first or the seventh. And if they are not in the angles, but
are above the earth, count from them up to the ASC. If there are
infortunes between them, they signify the number of elder brothers.
And look from the degree of the MC to the degree of the ASC. For if
there are fortunes between them, they signify that the native has
living brothers. But if there are malefics between the prior angles,
they signify that he had brothers, but they are already dead. But if
the fortunes are there, not the malefic stars, they signify that he
is the first born of his own mother.

After this, look in the same manner at the planets which are
between the ASC and the Angle of Earth. If they are benefics, the
mother will bear children again after him. But if they are malefics,
some will live, but many of them will be born prematurely.

And if there are no infortunes between them, the native's mother
will not bear any children after him that will live; and if there are
evil [planets], she will bear children that will die or will perish
in premature birth. Furthermore, if neither fortunes nor evil
[planets] are there, she will not bear [any] after him.

Next, look at the lord of the house of brothers. If it is in the
ASC or in the 7th house, he is an only child, that is one without
brothers. And if it is in the MC, he has brothers older than he is.
If in the Angle of Earth, he has a younger brother, and the brothers
before him are masculine.[56]

And if the lord of the house of brothers is joined to evil
[planets] or in aspect with them, it signifies the death and
destruction of them among themselves.[57] And if it is joined to
fortunes or in aspect with them, it signifies that the brothers will
endure and that there will be concord and joy among them.

Moreover, you will observe that the Sun and Saturn signify elder
brothers, Jupiter and Mars middle brothers, Mercury younger brothers,
the Moon elder sisters, and Venus younger sisters. And therefore if
the Sun and Saturn are impedited, it signifies the death of the elder
brothers; if Jupiter and Mars, of the middle brothers; if Mercury,
the younger [brothers]; if the Moon, the elder sisters; and if Venus,
the younger [sisters].

55. The printed text has *tertiae* 'third' instead of *terrae* 'earth', but this is corrected in the
Errata at the end of the book.
56. Here, "brother" and "brothers" are used in the sense of "siblings."
57. That is, they will slay each other.

The separation of the Moon from the Sun or from Saturn, signifies that the native has an elder brother; from Jupiter or from Mars, it signifies that he himself is not older than [all] his brothers; and from Venus, that the native has a sister older than himself; from Mercury and from Venus, he does not have a brother older than himself. And when the Moon is void of course, it signifies that the native's own brothers are in unhappy circumstances. And when it is separated from the fortunes, it signifies that the elder brothers will be happy and will lead happy lives. And if it is separated from evil [planets], it signifies quick death for the native's full brothers and the destruction of their possessions.

Chapt. 14. *The Reputation and Nobility of the Brothers.*

Know that the first lord[58] of the triplicity of the house of brothers signifies elder brothers; the second [lord], middle [brothers]; and the third, younger [brothers]. If one of these is in its own domicile or its own exaltation, free from [any aspect of] the evil [planets], in a suitable place in the circle [of houses] and from the Sun, it signifies the elevation of those brothers of which it is the significator. And the application of the lord of the 3rd house to a planet in exaltation or in its own domicile signifies that the brothers will be prosperous and will be associated with nobles and princes. But the application of it to a cadent planet or its conjunction with one in its fall signifies that the brothers will be worthless and will associate with worthless men.

The separation of the Moon from a planet in its own domicile, or posited in its exaltation, signifies that the elder brothers will have high position and great fame. And its application to a planet in its own domicile signifies that the native will be elevated and his name well-known, and that the one who is born after him will also be elevated.

But when you find the Head of the Dragon of the Moon in the house of brothers, it portends that the native will be of lesser condition and status than all of his brothers. And if the Tail [of the Dragon] is in the house of brothers, it signifies a happier status for the native than for his brothers.

And if the lord of the 3rd sign is a fortune, free from [any aspect of] the evil [planets], it signifies harmony among the brothers and good status for the native. But if they are evil [planets] and apply to malefics, it signifies destruction of the brothers and condemnation of the native's law.[59] Similarly, when a benefic star is in the house of brothers or in square or opposite

---

58. The printed text has *domus* 'house' instead of *dominus* 'lord'.

59. Here, and in the next two sentences, the phrase *legis nati* 'the native's law' occurs. This has reference to the native's degree of observance of the laws of behavior prescribed by his religion, and, by extension, to the degree of his faith in his religion. In the Islamic world of the 9th century, civil law and the accepted code of conduct were strongly rooted in religion. The reader may substitute "personal code of conduct" for "law" at this point in the text, for the 3rd house signifies the native's relations with those close to him -- his brothers and his neighbors. But compare the note at the beginning of Chapt. 29 below.

aspect to it, it signifies happiness of the brothers and goodness of
the native's law. And when there is an infortune in these places, it
signifies condemnation of the brothers' condition and of the native's
law.

Moreover, when you want to know whether the native is of greater
worth, or whether in fact his brothers are, look at the lords of the
triplicity of the ASC and the lords of the triplicity of the house of
his brothers, for whichever lords of the aforesaid houses are in a
better or more dignified place, that one will be of greater worth.
You will recall moreover that the first lord of the triplicity
signifies elder brothers, the second [lord] middle [brothers], and
the third younger [brothers]. Similarly, the Sun and Saturn signify
elder brothers, Jupiter and Mars middle [brothers], Mercury younger
[brothers], the Moon and Venus sisters, the former elder [sisters],
and the latter younger ones. Therefore, whichever of these planets or
of the lords of the triplicity of the 3rd house is stronger and more
fortunate and in a more dignified place, those whose significator it
is will be of greater worth among the brothers.

Chapt. 15. *The Mutual Friendship or Hatred of the Brothers.*

In this connection, look at the lord of the ASC and the lord of
the third sign. If they aspect each other mutually by trine or
sextile aspect, it signifies friendship with the brothers, but if by
square they will be middling in their friendship. And if by
opposition, it produces great enmity for and much hatred of the
brothers. And if they are conjoined, it signifies a stable friendship
with the brothers. Next, you will also look at the Part of Brothers
and at its place in the circle [of houses]. And if the lord of its
house aspects it by trine or sextile aspect, it signfies a firm
friendship. If it aspects it by square aspect, it signifies a
middling friendship. But if by opposition, it signifies great enmity
and hatred.

Know, moreover, that when the Part of Brothers is with the lord of
the Part of Fortune the brothers will contend among themselves with
mutual hatred and cheating and trickery. Mercury and Mars signify
brothers [as I have said], so when these [planets] are well and
harmoniously posited in relation to each other, then things relating
to brothers will work out more easily; but when there is no
application, the brothers' possessions will be divided and dispersed.

Venus and the Moon signify sisters. If they are harmonious and
joined by application, it will be good for things relating to
sisters. But if they are not in application, then the sisters'
possessions will be destroyed.

Chapt. 16. *The Fortune of the Parents, and the Things Signified by*
the Fourth House.

For the fortune of the parents, consider the place of the Sun in a
diurnal nativity and the place of Saturn in a nocturnal nativity. But
in a diurnal chart as well as in a nocturnal chart you will [also]

look at the Part of the Father⁶⁰ and its lord, and for both parents
the 4th sign from the ASC with its lord.

Next, as regards the mother, you will make your judgment from
Venus by day and the Moon by night, [and] both by day and by night
from the Part of the Mother⁶¹ and its lord. And if you find [all] the
significators of the father and the mother, or the majority of them,
having many aspects and dignities in the angles, or in the succedents
of the angles, and Fortuna is in the house of the father, and the
lords of the triplicity of that luminary which is the Lord of the
Time are happily posited in strong places in the circle [of houses],
it signifies prosperity for the parents and good circumstances and
much joy for them. But if they are impedited and in evil houses, it
signifies unhappy conditions for the parents and long-lasting
infirmity.

But if the Sun is in a suitable place in a day nativity, and the
lords of its triplicity are in evil houses, it signifies that the
father will be in prosperous circumstances at the time of the
nativity, but in unhappy circumstances in the future. [But] if the
same luminary is in an evil house, and the lords of its triplicity
are in good houses, it signifies bad conditions for the parents at
the time of the native's birth, but it indicates good [conditions] in
the future.

In general, the Sun in diurnal nativities with the Part of the
Father has signification over the condition of the father in the hour
of the nativity; and Saturn and the Part of the Father signify the
fortune of the father in nocturnal nativities. Therefore, direct the
degree of the Sun and the Part of the Father in diurnal nativities,
and the degree of Saturn and the Part of the Father in nocturnal
nativities, to the body of the fortunes and the malefics and to their
rays.

For if the aforesaid significators are conjoined with fortunes or
have *Alictisal*⁶² with them, it signifies elevation and happiness for
the father; and when they are conjoined by direction to the evil
[planets], or have *Alictisal* with them, it signifies infirmities and
other dangers that happen to the parents, but especially when they

---

60. Firmicus (*Mathesis*, VI.xxxii.3) gives us the formula: Saturn - Sun + ASC by day, and Sun -
Saturn + ASC by night. Dorotheus (*Pentateuch*, i.19) agrees, with the exception that he says to
subtract the planetary distance from the ASC in the case of a night birth. This is of course wrong,
since it would yield the same result as the day formula. Evidently the original formula said
"measure from planet A to planet B by day and add the result to the ASC, but by night the reverse."
Somewhere in the chain, Source - Dorotheus - Persian trans. - Arabic trans., the part of the
statement that said "by night the reverse" was taken to apply not just to the pair of planets, but
also to the direction of measurement from the ASC. Whether the error was committed by Dorotheus
himself or by one of his translators is uncertain. However, Ptolemy (*Tetrabiblos*, iii. 10) made the
same blunder.
61. Dorotheus (*Pentateuch*, i. 14) and Firmicus (*Mathesis*, VI.xxxii.21-22) give the formula: Moon
- Venus + ASC by day, and Venus - Moon + ASC by night. As with the Part of the Father, Dorotheus
mistakenly says to subtract the planetary distance from the ASC by night.
62. A technical term transliterated from the Arabic *al-ittiṣal* 'conjunction'. Sahl ibn Bishr
(*Introduction to the Science of Judgments of the Stars in Interrogations* i. 4) defines it as "a
light and swift planet going to conjunction with a slower and heavier planet."

become equal in degrees, and if, with the infortunes prevailing, the
fortunes do not project their rays there. Moreover, in such a
direction, when the Part of the Father and its lord are conjoined,
either by body or by rays, [the father] will come into much money.

And when Mercury is with Mars or when it aspects him with hostile
rays, it signifies an intensification of the hatred between the
brothers and the dishonesty, treachery, and deceit of one against
another.[63]

Also, the Part of the Father in good and strong houses from the
ASC and from the significator of the father -- either the Sun or
Saturn -- according to what the distinction of time[64] gives,
signifies an increase in honor for the father. But in houses from the
ASC, or from Saturn or the Sun, that are cadent, it signifies bad
circumstances for the father: servile poverty, contempt, and low
status. You will judge similarly about the mother's situation: by
day, from Venus and the Part of the Mother;[65] and by night from the
Moon and the Part of the Mother; just as I have made plain to you in
the signification of the father from the Sun and the rest of the
significators.

Look at the degree of the New Moon or the Full Moon most nearly
preceding the nativity. And if fortunes aspect it and the evil
[planets] are cadent from it, it signifies good circumstances for the
brothers and the parents and their elevation; but if the evil
[planets] aspect it and the fortunes have fallen away from it, the
contrary is signified. But if both fortunes and evil [planets] aspect
it at the same time, it signifies a middling status for them, and
especially if the Moon is in a fortunate position. And know that the
sign of the New Moon and its lord signify the fortune of the father,
and the sign of the Full Moon and its lord the fortune of the mother.

Besides this, look at the 4th sign, because if Jupiter or the Sun
is in it, or aspects it, it signifies the elevation of the father and
his great good fortune. And if Venus or the Moon is in it, or aspects
the sign, the elevation and high status of the mother is signified
and her good fortune. And if any one of the evil [planets] is in it
or aspects it, and the fortunes are not in aspect, then judge
servitude and misfortune and poverty for the native's parents. And if
that sign is the domicile or exaltation of the Sun, it signifies
servitude and misfortune for the father; but if it is the domicile of
the Moon or her exaltation, it signifies servitude for the mother and
that she is of low degree.

Furthermore, if the luminaries themselves are in mobile signs, it
signifies inconstancy for the parents and unsteady circumstances
along with a great variety of things. Also, you may know that the Sun
by day and Saturn by night signify the situation of the father at the

---

63. This paragraph seems out of place here. It would suit the theme of Chapt. 15. (It resembles
the first part of *Pentateuch* i.21.34.) But perhaps Abu 'Ali considered it appropriate to
discussion of the 4th house because the harmony or disharmony of the brothers affects the parents.
  64. That is, diurnal or nocturnal.
  65. The printed text has "Mars" instead of "Mother," corrected in the Errata at the end of the
book.

time of the nativity; and the lords of the domiciles of both these
significators signify the future fortunes of the father.

And when the significators of the father, which are the lord of
the domicile of the Sun in diurnal nativities and the lord[s] of its
triplicity are in their own exaltations, or the lord of the domicile
of Saturn in nocturnal nativities and the lords of its triplicity are
in their own exaltations, and in good houses of the figure, and the
Part of the Father, and its lord by night and by day, in their own
domiciles or exaltations, all of them free from [any aspect of] the
infortunes, with an aspect of the fortunes, it signifies the
elevation and high dignity and an abundance of wealth for the parents
of the native, and especially if the Part of Fortune and its lord are
both fortunately placed along with the Part of the Father, for then
it also signifies that the father's good fortune will endure, and the
son will come into a sumptuous inheritance left [to him] by his
parents.

But contrariwise, if the lord of the domicile of the Sun in a
diurnal nativity and the lord of its triplicity, or the lord of the
domicile of Saturn in nocturnal nativities and the lord of its
triplicity are in evil houses, or in their detriment, or in their own
fall configured with the evil [planets], it signifies the downfall of
the father and the loss of his assets.

Look further into the value and worth of the family[66] and of their
success in riches and dignities from the *Ductoria*[67] of the diurnal
planets from the Sun and of the nocturnal planets from Saturn. And if
you find any one of them in its own *Ductoria*, it will signify
increase and elevation and enlargement of the honor and worth of the
family in the future.

Similar is the judgment on the fortune of the mother from the
Ductoria of the nocturnal planets and from the Moon. And if any one
of them is in itw own *Ductoria*, it denotes the elevation of the
mother and her importance and an increase in dignity for her in the
future.

Besides all this, in judging the status of the family, look at the
Sun by day and its lord and the lord of its triplicity; or, if the
nativity is nocturnal, at Saturn and the lord of its domicile and the
lords of its triplicity. For if the Sun and the Moon and the lords of
the aforesaid domiciles and the lords of the triplicities are in
angles, free from [any aspects with] the evil [planets] and from
detriments, it signifies joy and prosperity for the native and his
family. But if [these significators] are discovered to be impedited
and conjoined to the evil [planets], not in aspect with the ASC, and
cadent, it signifies an unhappy status and death for the native as
well as for his family.

---

66. Here, "family" means the native's father's extended family and its place and standing in the
community.
67. A technical term transliterated from the Arabic *dusturiya* from a Middle Persian word
signifying a position of power.

38   ABU 'ALI AL-KHAYYAT

Chapt. 17. *The Length of Life of the Father.*

Ptolemy said,[68] Look at the Sun when the nativity is by day. If it aspects the ASC, direct it to the body and the rays of the infortunes by the degrees of ascension, giving to each degree of ascension one year.[69] And if the Sun does not aspect the ASC, but Saturn does aspect it, direct it instead of the Sun; but if it does not aspect the Sun either, [then] in place of these direct the degree of the Angle of Earth.

In nocturnal nativities you will begin with Saturn, after it the Sun, and after the Sun the degree of the IMC. Then look at how many years result from the degrees of the ascensions. Which, if it is as many as those that that planet signifies, which has the greater dignity by day in the place of the Sun and in the lord of its domicile, and by day and by night equally, in the 4th house and its lord, but by night in Saturn and in the lord of its domicile, and the Part of the Father and its lord,[70] or if the number of degrees of ascension was nearly equal to the years of that planet, his father will die in the same year.[71]

Chapt. 18. *The Length of Life of the Mother.*

Ptolemy said,[72] In the case of the mother, when the nativity is diurnal, look at Venus. If it aspects the ASC, direct it to the body and the rays of the evil [planets] by the degrees of ascension, and give one year to each degree of ascension. And if it does not aspect the ASC, but the Moon is sending rays to it, direct her just as we said about Venus. But if the Moon does not aspect the ASC either, [then] direct the degree of the MC.

But in nocturnal nativities begin with the Moon, then Venus, and finally the degree of the MC. Then consider how many years result from the degrees of the ascensions. For if there are as many degrees as that planet signified which has the greater dignity by day in the place of Venus, or by night in the place of the Moon and in the lord of its domicile, or by day and by night equally in the degree of the MC and its lord, and in the Part of the Mother and its lord, or if the degrees of ascension found by the direction was nearly equal to its number of years, the death of the mother is signified in that year.

---

68. This presumably refers to *Tetrabiblos*, iii. 4 "Of Parents," although the specific instructions given by Abu 'Ali are mostly different from those given by Ptolemy. But perhaps the reference is to one of the numerous other works falsely attributed to Ptolemy.

69. That is, by using primary zodiacal directions.

70. I have translated this long, awkward sentence as it appears in the printed text. Its exact meaning is uncertain. Perhaps the most likely interpretation is that the astrologer should determine which of the significators (the Sun, its lord, a planet in the 4th house, the lord of the 4th house, etc.) is the most dignified.

71. He means that if there is a near or exact coincidence between the number of degrees in the primary arc and the number of years signified by the planet (See the table in Chapt. 4), then the father may be expected to live that many years. This is an example of reinforcement of an indication by duplication. See the final *Caution* following Chapt. 50.

72. See the preceding note.

Chapt. 19. *Finding the Hyleg for the Life of the Parents.*

Look at the Sun in diurnal nativities. If it is in an angular or succeding sign and any one of the lords of the five dignities aspects it, the Sun will be the Hyleg, which you will direct for the father, and the planet that is lord of the dignity and aspecting the Sun will be the Alcochoden, through which is known the [number of] years of the father's life.

But if the Sun is not [posited] as we have said, and Saturn is in an angle or a succedent of an angle, and one of the lords of the five dignities aspects it, [then] Saturn will be the Hyleg, which you will direct for the father, and the planet that is the lord of the dignity and in aspect will be the Alcochoden.

But then, if Saturn is not configured in the aforesaid manner, look at the degree of the Part of the Father. If it is in an angle or a succedent of an angle, and any one of the lords of the five dignities aspects it, [then] the Part of the Father will be the Hyleg, which you will direct for the father, and the lord of the dignity -- namely, the planet in aspect, will be the Alcochoden.

But if the Part was not [configured] as we have said, look at the degree of the house of the father,[73] because if any one of the lords of the five dignities aspects it, [then] that degree will be the Hyleg, and it must be directed for the life of the father, and the planet in aspect that is lord of the dignity will be the Alcochoden.

In the same manner, begin in nocturnal nativities with Saturn, then with the Sun, then with the Part of the Father, and finally with the degree of the house of the father, and use the same method that we have given previously.

Furthermore, in investigating the life of the mother, you will begin with Venus in diurnal nativities, then with the Moon, then with the Part of the Mother, and after these with the degree of the MC. And in nocturnal nativities, you will begin with the Moon, then with Venus, then with the Part of the Mother, and finally with the degree of the MC. And whichever of these is the more dignified according to the rules given above will be the Hyleg, which ought to be directed for the life of the mother, and the lord of the dignity in aspect will be the Alcochoden as above. And if you don't find a Hyleg, direct the degree of the Moon to the fortunes and to the evil planets] to explore the status of the mother, assigning one year to each degree. Also, you will know the fortune of the mother from that planet from which the Moon [last] separated.

---

73. That is, the IMC degree.

Chapt. 20. *The Status of the Children, and the Things Signified by
the Fifth House.*

For this, look at the house of children and its lord, and at Venus
and Jupiter, and also the Part of Children[74] and its lord, and the
lord of the triplicity of Jupiter. For whichever one of these is the
most dignified in a sign of many children, free from [any aspect of]
the evil [planets], aspecting the ASC, and especially if it is in an
angle or a succedent of an angle, signifies many children. And if it
is in a sign signifying few children, impedited by evil [planets],
and Jupiter is combust, and Venus impedited, it signifies that the
native will be barren and will never have children. And if the lord
of the ASC is applied to the lord of the 7th, it signifies many
children that are not legitimate. And if the lord of the 7th applies
to the lord of the ASC, it signifies many from slave-girls. And say
that many children [are signified] by Jupiter and Venus, few by
Saturn and Mars, and a middling number by the Sun, the Moon, and
Mercury.

But if the lords of the triplicity of Jupiter are in good places
in the circle, it signifies many children and joy from them. But if
one of them is in a suitable place and the others in dejected or evil
[places], it signifies that the native will have one child that is
outstanding and honored. But sorrow will come to him from the rest of
his children, because if the lords of the triplicity of Jupiter are
cadent from the angles or under the Sun beams, few children are
indicated.

Besides this, if Jupiter and Mercury are in their own domiciles or
exaltations, in angles or succedents of angles, and the lords of
their triplicities are in suitable places in the circle, free from
[any aspect of] the evil [planets] and from impediments, it signifies
many children and joy from them. And look at the Part of Children and
its lord, and the planet conjoined to it, or the star configured with
it, and judge the fortune of the children according to the measure of
the houses and their quality in strength and weakness.

And know that when the Part of Children is in an angle or the
succedent of an angle, it signifies many children and harmony [among
them]. And if it is cadent from the angles, and especially [if it is]
in those houses that do not aspect the ASC,[75] it signifies few
children and their quick demise. Besides, if the Part of Children
does not aspect good planets, it signifies the death of the first-
born child, who perhaps may be born dead; and the native will always
have sorrow from his children. But if there is a fortune in square or
opposite aspect to the Part of Children, it signifies many children.
But if an evil [planet] beholds it with the same aspects, it
signifies few children and little joy from them. And if Venus is
impedited by Saturn, look at the Part of Children. And if it is in a

74. Al-Biruni (*The Book of Instruction*, Sect. 476) gives the formula: Saturn - Jupiter + ASC by
day, and Jupiter - Saturn + ASC by night. As with most of the Parts, Dorotheus (*Pentateuch*, ii. 10)
mistakenly says to subtract the planetary distance from the ASC by night. Firmicus (*Mathesis*
VI.xxxii.33-35) uses Mercury and Venus and gives special rules for their sequence.
75. The 2nd, 6th, 8th, and 12th houses.

angle, and does not aspect either Jupiter or Venus, it signifies few children and barenness, especially if the Moon is also impedited.

And if Jupiter, Venus, and Mercury are free from [any aspect of] the evil [planets], free from retrogradation, and free from combustion, the native will be the father of many children. But if they are impedited by the evil [planets], or in their detriment, or in their fall, or under the Sun beams, he will have no children; and if he does have any, they will die.

And if a fortune is in the 5th sign, and the lord of the house of children is free from [any aspect of] the evil [planets] and free from impediments, and aspecting the MC, it signifies that the native will have many children who will get along very well together. Conversely, if there is an evil planet in the house of children, and the lord of the house of children is falling from an angle, it signifies few children and the swift death of one of them, and especially if it is cadent from the 4th or the 7th angle. And in all nativities, if the luminaries are impedited by evil [planets], and no fortune aspects them, it signifies few children and little money. Wherefore, if you have rightly understood and considered all these things, you will discover the truth of the matter, if God wills.

Chapt. 21. *The Time of the Children.*

For the time of the children, look at the planet which is most dignified in the significations of children. If it is oriental, it signifies children in [the native's] youth; if it is occidental, in his old age; if it is in the MC or the 11th sign, it promises children in youth; if it is in the 3rd, 9th, or 4th house, it signifies children in mid-life. Also, if the Part of Children is in the ASC, it signifies children in youth; if in the MC, children in youth. If the Part of Children is in the 7th or 4th house, it will give children at the end of life. And when in the revolution of years[76] Jupiter or Venus comes to the place of the Part of Children or aspects it by square or opposition, it signifies that he will have children at that time. (Jupiter has a greater signification for children than does Venus.)

Similarly, when the profection of the year[77] comes to the sign in which Jupiter or Venus is placed in the nativity, it signifies children in that year.

If you want to know the love and concord [that will exist] among the children and their goodwill towards the native, look at the planet that is most dignified in the significations of children and the lord of the ASC. If they are in good mutual aspect or in reception, it signifies concord and happiness from the children. But

---

76. That is, the *solar return*, as it is called nowadays.
77. An ancient method of prediction set forth, for example, by Paul of Alexandria in his *Introduction to Astrology*, Chapt. 31. See also William Lilly's *Christian Astrology*, pp. 715-734. The yearly profection begins with the ASC and moves forward in the zodiac 30° per year, thus performing a revolution in 12 years. Refer to the sources mentioned for technical details of its use.

if they are configured with mutual impediments, it signifies discord
and enmity of the children towards the native and harm [to him].

Similarly, if the Part of Children receives a friendly aspect from
its lord, especially if the Part of Children is not impedited and its
lord is a fortune, it is a true sign of sincere love between the
native and his children, and this the more if the Part of Children
and its lord aspect the ASC and its lord with friendly rays. If the
lord of the 1st house is in the 5th, or the lord of the 5th or the
Part of Children is in it, it signifies perfect love between the
native and his children. But if you find the lord of the 5th, the
Part of Children, or its lord in the 7th house, [the children] will
be open enemies and adversaries of their father. Similarly, if the
lord of the 5th house, the Part of Children, or its lord are found in
the 12th, the children will be secret enemies of the native. If the
lord of the 1st is in the 2nd, 8th, or 12th house, the native will
hate his children and turn them away. The Part of Life[78] and its lord
also cause this when they are posited in these three houses, unless a
stronger contrary testimony by the lords of either the 1st or the 5th
house is in effect.

Chapt. 22. *The Native's Slaves and Subordinates, and the Significations of the Sixth House.*

For the circumstances of slaves, subordinates,[79] and captives,
look at the 6th sign and its lord and its place in the circle, and
[see] besides if any one of the benefics or malefics is in the 6th
house, or the Part of Captives,[80] also the place of Mercury, because
through that is known its signification over slaves, subordinates,
and captives, and [Mercury's] better condition is when it is oriental
in the ASC or in the MC applying to Jupiter, in a common or mobile
sign. When any one of the fortunes is in the 6th sign or the 12th, or
the lord of the 6th is a fortune, free from [any aspect of] the evil
[planets], and conjoined to Mercury, or if Mercury is joined to the
fortunes or applies to them free from [any aspect of] the evil
[planets], or its lord is in a suitable house, and the fortunes
aspect it and the infortunes are falling away from it, it signifies
many slaves and advantage and joy accruing [to the native] from them.

But truly the very worst condition for Mercury is when it is
retrograde, or under the Sun beams, or conjoined to the evil
[planets], or applying to them in a fixed sign, because if there is
any one of the evil [planets] in the 6th sign or the 12th, or the

---

78. Al-Biruni (*The Book of Instruction*, Sect. 476) gives the formula: Saturn - Jupiter + ASC by
day and Jupiter - Saturn + ASC by night.
79. Literally, "those subject to the native" -- i.e., those who must do his bidding, but who are
not slaves or captives.
80. There is some question here as to which Part Abu 'Ali had in mind. Al-Biruni (*The Book of
Instruction*, Sect. 476) lists a Part of Captivity with the formula: Ruler of the Sun's sign - Sun +
ASC by day, and Ruler of the Moon's sign - Moon + ASC by night. The first part of the formula is
reversed by two later writers. Ibn Ezra (*The Beginning of Wisdom*, Chapt. 9) has a Part of Prison
and Captivity, whose formula is Sun - Ruler of the Sun's sign + ASC by day and Moon - Ruler of the
Moon's sign + ASC by night. Leopold of Austria (*Compilation of the Science of the Stars*, iv. 5)
gives the same formula and calls it the Part of Captives.

lord of the 6th is an evil planet or a planet impedited by the Sun in
an evil place in the circle, or if Mercury is impedited by evil
[planets] or is falling away from the fortunate stars and they are
not aspecting it, or if the Part of Slaves[1] itself is impedited by
the evil [planets] and lacks any aspect of the fortunes, or if the
Tail of the Dragon of the Moon is found in the 6th house, it
signifies few slaves and sorrow accruing [to the native] from them.

     For the circumstances of captives and slaves, look too at the star
that is most dignified in the place of the lord of the 6th, and [in
the place of] the Part of Captives, and its lord, and [look at]
Mercury, and the star that is in the 6th house, whether there is one
or more, and its relationship or harmony with the lord of the ASC,
and whether it makes the latter fortunate or unfortunate. And judge,
just as you see it, about the [slaves'] utility or inutility, or
about their benefit or loss [to the native]. So, consider the many
[testimonies], and ponder diligently the utility, discord, benefit,
or impediment that the native will get from his slaves.

     See also the planet which has the most points of dignity in the
6th house, and the lord of the 6th, and the Part of Slaves and its
lord, and the planet which is in the 6th, and Mercury and the lord of
the ASC, for if one of these makes another fortunate, it signifies
agreement and success, but if one impedites another, their discord
and impediment are signified. And keep on looking at the multitude of
testimonies until the true state of the matter becomes apparent to
you.

Chapt. 23. *The Native's Luck with Animals and Cattle.*

     In regard to animals and cattle, look at the 12th sign and its
lord, and Mars and its place in the circle, and its individual
condition, that is, whether it is oriental or occidental, retrograde
or direct. And know that in the case of animals it is better for Mars
to be oriental in a quadrupedal sign, and especially in a regal sign
in the ASC or the MC, or [even] in the 12th, because if you find it
so and Jupiter and the Sun aspect it with a benign aspect, it
signifies that the native will have many animals and cattle,
especially if Mars is in a house or sign where it has some dignity.
And when Mars is with the Part of Fortune, it signifies that the
native will love horses, weapons, and hunting, especially if the Moon
is with it and Mars is lord of the ASC or lord of the conjunction or
opposition of the luminaries that was [immediately] before the
nativity.

     But when the 12th sign is quadrupedal and its lord is in a
quadrupedal sign conjoined to the fortunes, or in aspect with them,
it signifies that the native will have advantage from animals and
cattle, and they will multiply around him. But if the 12th is a fixed
sign and Saturn is in it or in square aspect or in opposition, it
signifies that sorrow and impediment will happen to the native; and
this will be through animals and cattle if Jupiter and Mars have

---

81. Al-Biruni, Ibn Ezra, and Leopold agree on the formula for this Part: Moon - Mercury + ASC by
day and by night.

particular dignity in the same sign. And know that if Mars is
oriental in Aries, Leo, or Sagittarius, and it is the lord of the 6th
or the 12th sign, it promises to the native many animals, viz.
horses, camels, and [other] large animals of great value, especially
if Jupiter aspects it. And if it is in Taurus, or Virgo, or
Capricorn, it signifies that the native will have many draft-animals
or beasts of burden, such as cattle and cows and such like. And
similarly with the other signs, when Mars is in them oriental,
conjoined to the fortunes or in aspect with them, it signifies
advantage from animals according to the nature of the sign in which
Mars is placed. And if Sagittarius or any of the signs of a bestial
nature is ascending, and the lord of the ASC is with Mars or in
aspect with it from praiseworthy houses, the native will love animals
and derive pleasure from them. Similarly, if the Moon is in the
places that I have just named for the lord of the ASC, it will
signify just as much as the lord of the ASC, if God wills.

Chapt. 24. *The Native's Infirmity and its Causes.*

With regard to the occurrences of infirmities and their causes and
kinds, consider the 6th sign and its lord, and the Part of
Infirmities[82] along with its lord, and the planets that are in it,
whether fortunes or malefics, and also the Moon, and the lord of her
domicile, because she has the greatest signification in infirmities.
But if the majority of them are fortunes, or if any one of them has
more testimonies of dignity and is fortunately placed and configured
with the lord of the ASC, it signifies that the native will be
healthy and that he will have [only] minor infirmities and few [of
these]. But if the majority of them are evil [planets], and any one
of them has greater dignity, but is still impeded by the evil
[planets] and configured with the lord of the ASC, it signifies that
the native will have a variety of sicknesses, especially if it is in
any of the angles or the succedents of the angles.

But if Saturn is more dignified that the others, or if the planet
that is stonger than the rest is impeded by Saturn, it signifies
many maladies, viz. paralysis, hemorrhoids, dropsy, and all
infirmities that are cold and dry and difficult to cure. And if Mars
is the most dignified of them, or if the one that has the most
dignities is impeded by Mars, it signifies hot maladies, from
choler, and from blood, or fevers, delirium, and apoplexy.

And if Saturn is in the 6th sign from the ASC or from the Moon, or
in square aspect or in opposition to these places, it signifies many
cold sicknesses, especially if it is in a moist sign. But if Mars is
in such a position, it signifies that the native will have many hot
infirmities, from which he will either be quickly liberated or will
quickly die.

And if the Moon and its lord and the 6th sign are free from
impediments and the [aspects of] the evil [planets], it signifies
that the native will be healthy; but if, on the contrary, they are

---

82. Al-Biruni, Ibn Ezra, and Leopold give the formula for this Part: Mars - Saturn + ASC by day,
and Saturn - Mars + ASC by night.

impedited, it signifies his death and many infirmities. And if an evil [planet] is in the ASC, especially Mars in a nocturnal nativity, and it is conjoined to the Moon, it signifies weakness of sight and the destruction of an eye. Similarly, if the luminaries are impedited by the evil [planets], or are joined to the Tail of the Dragon of the Moon, weakness of sight is signified and the destruction of the eyes. For if the Moon is conjoined to the evil [planets] by square aspect or by opposition, and it is in a moist sign, it signifies that the native's many infirmities will be from cold and moisture. And if it is in a dry sign, with these same conditions, it signifies illnesses from heat and dryness.

And if the planet that signifies infirmity is oriental, the infirmities will be in the beginning of the native's life. But if it is occidental, they will be in the end of his life. If it is in the ASC, they will happen in the beginning of life; if in the MC, they will happen in the middle of life; if in the Angle of Earth, they will happen around the end. But in any case the native's infirmities will be in accordance with the essential strength or weakness of the planet. And when the Part of Infirmity and its lord are free from [any aspect of] the evil [planets], it promises that the native will be sound and his body healthy. But if they are impedited, it threatens pains and the most severe tortures, but especially if no fortune aspects them.

In general, the ASC and the Moon are significators of the body, and the lord of the ASC and the lord of the Moon's domicile are significators of the mind. If therefore the ASC and the Moon are impedited, but their lords are free from [any aspect of] the evil [planets], it signifies some weakness of the native's body, but soundness of his mind and judgment. And if the ASC and the Moon are free from [any aspect of] the evil [planets] but their lords are impedited, it signifies soundness of the body but sickness and terror and sadness of the mind.

Chapt. 25. *Matrimonial Matters and their Causes, and the Things Signified by the Seventh House.*

Make your judgment of matters relating to matrimony and marriage[83] from the 7th sign and its lord and from the planet that you find in the 7th domicile of heaven, also from Venus and the Moon, and from

---

83. The printed text has *desponsationis*, which in Classical Latin means 'betrothal', but the context suggests that the subject is "marriage and its aftermath," not "betrothal." (The Spanish word *desposar* means 'to marry', and this may have influenced the choice of *desponsatio* as its supposed Latin equivalent.) In what follows I have translated *desponsatio* as 'marriage'. However, I think the author is drawing a distinction between the "act of marriage" and the "state of wedlock" that follows marriage.

the Part of Marriage[84] and its lord. If all of these significators, or those of them that are the most powerful, have dignities in the angles or in the succedents, free from [any aspect of] the evil [planets], free from combustion, and applying to the lord of the ASC, it signifies that the native will have a good and suitable marriage. But if the lord of the ASC applies to the lord of the 7th sign, it signifies that the native has the desire to acquire wives.[85] And contrariwise, if the lord of the 7th house applies to the lord of the ASC, it signifies that the native will be sought and esteemed by women. And if Venus is direct in an angle or a succedent, fortunately configured, and not impedited, and the lords of its triplicity are oriental in favorable houses and free from impediment, it signifies that the native will marry in his youth, and he will be fortunate [in his relations] with his wives. But if Venus is cadent or combust, and the lords of its triplicity are in abject houses, and in aspect with the evil [planets], it signifies a late marriage for the native and inconveniences from causes relating to his wives.

And if Venus is in an angle or a succedent, free from [any aspect of] the evil [planets], and the lords of its triplicity are in evil houses, Venus signifies a good and agreeable marriage for the native, but the lords of its triplicity [signify] disadvantage and hard work from the [ensuing] wedlock.[86] And if Venus is impedited or cadent, and the lords of its triplicity are in favorable houses, the place of Venus signifies something malignant in the marriage, but the lords of the triplicity signify joy and advantage arising from his wives [in some manner].

And if Venus, in the nativities or women or men, is free from [any aspect of] the evil [planets] and free from impediments, and in suitable houses, it signifies an advantageous and good marriage. But if it is impedited in an evil house, it signifies disadvantage and something malignant in the marriage. But when Venus is in a mobile sign, it signifies little stability of the native in wedlock, and fickle passions, especially if it is in Cancer or Capricorn. If this same [planet] is in opposition to the Moon or in square aspect to her, it signifies some impediment in the marriage. And if it is in a

---

84. Firmicus (Mathesis, VI.xxxii.27-31), Al-Biruni (loc. cit.), Ibn Ezra (loc. cit.), and Leopold (loc. cit.) give the formula: Venus - Saturn + ASC by day, and Saturn - Venus + ASC by night. This is the Part of Marriage for Men; for Women, the sequence of the planets is reversed. Dorotheus (Pentateuch, ii. 2-3) has the same two Parts, but he says the first one is for women, and the reverse for men, and makes his usual mistake in the case of nocturnal births. Although Dorotheus is our oldest authority, the agreement of Firmicus with the three medieval authors seems to me to tip the scales against Dorotheus. But this is surmise. To make matters worse, several other Parts relating to marriage are offered by each of these authorities, and Abu 'Ali may well have had a different Part in mind.

85. Here and in what follows I have sometimes translated the Latin word mulier as 'wife' and sometimes as 'woman'. Presumably, the Arabic original used the word imra'a 'woman', which, like the Lat. mulier, Span. mujer, and Fr. femme can mean 'woman' or 'wife' according to the context. In English the use of 'woman' for 'wife' is substandard, but it is acceptable or customary in the other languages mentioned. (The reader should also recall that a Muslim could marry as many wives as he wanted and could afford.)

86. Here, Abu 'Ali clearly illustrates a fundamental principle in horoscopic interpretation: contrary influences do not cancel each other out.

common sign (of two bodies, or of two faces or forms), it signifies
marriage of the native with two women.

When Venus is in a domicile of Mars and Mars is in a domicile of
Venus, it signifies an abundance of wives. But if it is in a domicile
of Saturn and Saturn is in her domicile, or when Venus is in a
domicile of Mercury and Mercury is in her domicile, or if Venus and
Mercury are in a domcile of Saturn, it shows that the native will
delight more in masculine intercourse than in feminine. And if any
one of the evil [planets] is in the 7th or in in the 4th house in the
nativities of men, it signifies the death of his wives; and in the
nativities of women, the death of their husbands. And when Venus is
peregrine and occidental, conjoined to the evil [planets], or in bad
aspect with them, it signifies the swift death of his wives.

Chapt. 26. *The Things Signified by the Part of Marriage.*

Consider the Part of Marriage and its lord. If they are in angles
or in succedents, free from [any aspect of] the evil [planets],
adjoined to the fortunes, or in aspect with the fortunes, it
signifies the marriage of the native with the best and most beautiful
women. And if the Part and its lord are cadent and impedited by the
evil [planets], but especially without any aspect of the fortunes to
them, it signifies the marriage of the native with infamous whores.
But if the lord of the Part of Fortune is direct in its course in an
angle or a succedent, free from [any aspect of] the evil [planets],
it signifies the marriage of the native with beautiful women and
those of the best [quality].

And if the lord of the Part of Fortune is evil, cadent,
retrograde, or combust, it signifies the marriage of the native with
women who are full of faults and who will bear no offspring. And if
Venus is cadent from the ASC, conjoined to Saturn, or in evil aspect
with Jupiter, it signifies that he native will have depraved
inclinations with regard to women. And if the lord of the 7th and the
lord of the Moon's domicile do not aspect the Moon, and the lord of
the Part of Marriage does not aspect the Part, and the lord of the
domicile of Venus does not aspect her, it signifies depravity of the
native's inclinations with regard to marriage and desire. Moreover,
when Saturn is elevated above Venus in the 10th sign or is in
opposition to her, it signifies that the native will have little love
for his wives.

When Venus is joined to Mars or in evil aspect with him, it
signifies the disgrace of sexual license. And when she is in a
domicile of Jupiter and in aspect with him in the nativities of men
or women, it signifies the suitability and accomplishment of marriage
and constancy in it. But when Venus is in a domicile of Mars, and in
aspect with him, it signifies condemnation and evil qualities in the
marriage partner. But when she is in her own domicile or exaltation,
or in the domicile of the Moon or in her exaltation, it signifies
marriage and connection of the native with women who live in his
neighborhood. And if you find Venus in a domicile of Jupiter, or
contrariwise, Jupiter in a domicile of Venus, it signifies marriage
with women of noble birth. And if Venus is in a domicile of Saturn,
it signifies marriage with an aged woman. And if she is in a domicile

of Mercury, it signifies connection with a low-born, common sort of
wife or with a slave-girl. If she is found in the domicile of the
Moon, it indicates marriage with an unsuitable woman. But if she is
in her own domicile or exaltation, or in an angle free from [any
aspect of] the evil [planets] and free from retrogradation and
combustion, it signifies a high-class marriage and good circumstances
for the native, especially if Jupiter aspects her. And if Venus is
oriental, it signifies that the wife will act boldly towards her
husband but with much love and joy. And if she is occidental or in
her own fall, it signifies little love between the native and his
wife, especially if Jupiter does not aspect her; and if she is
retrograde, it signifies that the native will have delay and
difficulty in getting married. When Venus is under the Sun beams, it
signifies marriage with women who are sick, and especially in
secret.[87]

And when the profection[88] of the year of the ASC of the radix
comes to the 7th sign, or the ASC of the revolution is the sign of
the 7th house, it signifies marriage in that year. And if that sign
is a mobile sign, it signifies marriage with many women; and if it is
common, with two; if fixed, with one. Understand all this, and you
will find the truth, if God is willing.

Chapt. 27. *The Native's Travel and Trips, and the Things Signified by the Ninth House.*

For the native's travel and trips, look at the 9th sign and its
lord and the planet that is in the 9th house. Also, [look at] Mars
and the Part of Travel[89] and its lord. For if most of these are
fortunes, or the one of them that has the greatest dignity there is
fortunately placed, applying to the lord of the ASC, or the lord of
the ASC applying to it, it signifies great profit and advantage from
travel. And if most of them are impedited, or they are rendered
unfortunate by the evil [planets], or the planet that has the
greatest dignity there is impedited or is an infortune, and it
applies to the lord of the ASC, it signifies that he will have bad
luck, loss, and damage from travel.

After that, see which one of them has the most testimonies and is
in the strongest place. If there is application and mutual
configuration between it and the lord of the ASC, along with mutual
harmony, it signifies that the native will make many trips. And if
there is no application, configuration, or harmony between them, it
signifies that the native will remain in his own place, loving joy
and quiet. And if Mars is in the ascending angle, it signifies travel
and many trips. And if the Moon does not aspect the lord of its
domicile, it signifies that the native will be one who finds his
livelihood outside his own native country.

---

87. Or perhaps Abu 'Ali means "especially when the planet is invisible."
88. The printed text has *perfectio* 'perfection' in error.
89. Al-Biruni, Ibn Ezra, and Leopold give the formula: Cusp of the 9th - Lord of the 9th + ASC
by day and by night. Firmicus (*Mathesis* VI.xxxii.49) offers a different formula.

Besides this, look at the lords of the triplicity of Mars, because the one that has the best condition and house [position] signifies that the native will have fortunate trips if it is itself fortunately placed, but unfortunate [trips] if it is unfortunately placed -- indeed, that the native will never get the sought for livelihood from his trips,⁹⁰ and in particular, [if it is] the first lord [of the triplicity] rather than the rest. And if the lord of the 9th sign is impedited, or if evil [planets] are in it, or if they apply to the lord of the ASC, or if the lord of the ASC applies to them, it signifies loss, bad luck, and disadvantage arising from [the native's] trips. But when the lord of the 9th house applies to Mars, or is in his domicile or terms, or aspects those terms,⁹¹ it signifies many and varied trips and dwelling in foreign regions.

Besides this, look at the [place of the] Moon on the third day of the nativity.⁹² If it is configured with Mars, or in his domicile, or in his terms, it signifies travel and many trips. But when the lord of the ASC is conjoined or in opposition to the place of the ASC, or in a sign of contrary nature to the ascending sign, and the lord of the domicile of the Moon is conjoined to the Moon, and if the lord of the ASC is in its own fall, it signifies that the native's livelihood will be in foreign regions. But if the lord of the domicile of the Sun is contrary to the Moon, it signifies that the native will carry through, i.e. he will complete many trips. And if it is a fortune, he will gain benefit and advantage from his trips; but if it is an evil [planet], something bad.

And if the Moon is in the 3rd sign from the ASC, applying to Mercury, and she herself is impedited by Mars, misfortunes will happen to the native on his trips. Moreover, if the Moon or the lord of her domicile is in the angle of the West, it signifies that the native will delight in trips. Similarly, if the lord of the ASC is in the 9th, or the lord of the 9th is in the ASC, it signifies the native's desire for trips and that he will move about from region to region. But when the Moon, on the third day of the nativity is applied to a fortune, and that fortune is oriental in a good house, it signifies that the native will profit from his trips. And if she is applied to an occidental infortune, which she does not receive, it signifies that the native will have loss and misfortune from his trips.

Chapt. 28. *Utility or Loss on a Trip.*

Look at the 9th sign. If there is a fortune in it, or in square aspect, or in opposition to it, it signifies joy and profit on trips, especially if the lord of the ASC is a fortune, or in aspect with the fortunes. But if an evil [planet] is in the 9th, or in square aspect, or in opposition to it, it signifies evil and loss from trips. But if the lord of the 9th is in the ASC or the MC, it signifies the native's love of and pleasure in trips. But if Venus is the lord of

---

90. The printed text ends the sentence at this point and begins a new one erroneously, as it seems.

91. This last clause is suspicious.

92. He means the second day after the nativity.

the 9th and it is located in the ASC or the MC, it signifies joy and marriage for the native while he is on a trip. And if Jupiter is lord of the 9th and placed in the ASC or the MC, it signifies the acquisition of a principate and [even] of an empire while on a trip.⁹³ And if Mercury is lord of the 9th [and posited] in the ASC or the MC, it signifies the acquisition of knowledge, and greatness, and the business affairs of nobles⁹⁴ while on a trip. But if Saturn is lord of the 9th and posited in the ASC or the MC, aspecting Jupiter, it signifies that [the native] will make a beneficial acquisition, while on a trip, of aquatic and terrestrial things and animals. And if Mars is lord of the 9th and is found in the ASC or the MC, aspecting Jupiter, he will gain something beneficial, while on a trip, from women and nobles and princes, to whom [the direction of] wars and armies are entrusted. But if the lord of the domicile of the Sun does not aspect the Sun, and the lord of the domicile of the Moon does not aspect the Moon, and the lord of the ASC does not behold the ASC, or if Mars is in the 3rd or 9th house, or the Part of Travel is with Mars, and the lord of the Part is of a nature contrary to its own house, it signifies many trips, [accompanied] by hard work, loss, and fear. And if the Part of Travel is in any of the angles, conjoined to the lord of the ASC or to the Moon, it signifies love affairs on trips.

Chapt. 29. *The Native's Law and Religion, and his Dreams.*

In matters of faith and dreams, look at the two houses, the 3rd and the 9th, because from them is known [the native's] law⁹⁵ and dreams. Therefore, you should know their strengths, and which planets are in them, or which aspect them, and which are the lords of the domicile, exaltation, triplicity, and terms, and in which house of the circle they are located. Also, which one is the lord of the Part of Law,⁹⁶ and in which house the Part [itself] is located, whether it is in a mobile sign or one of two bodies or a fixed [sign], or whether it is in an angle or a succedent or a cadent [house], whether its lord is oriental or occidental, direct or retrograde, under the Sun beams or beyond them. You will also observe that Mercury has its own proper signification in matters of faith and dreams, moreso than the others. Wherefore, see which of the planets it is configured with, or to which it applies, and which brings the most dignity to it.

---

93. Something like this happened to Aulus Vitellius (15-69). He arrived in Germany in November 68 to take charge of the army units there. Six weeks later, on 2 Jan 69, his men saluted him as Emperor of Rome. Unfortunately, we do not know the hour of his birth.

94. Or perhaps, 'the lawsuits of nobles'.

95. Here again, as in Chapt. 14, the phrase "the native's law" occurs. But now the emphasis is upon faith and religious observance as indicated in the horoscope. In Abu 'Ali's day, the civil law in Muslim lands was mainly based upon the Qu'ran and the Traditions. Likewise, the laws of the Jews within their own society were based upon their religion. Respect for and observance of the law arose naturally from respect for and observance of the religion that underlay it. Hence, "the native's law" means "the law prescribed by the native's religion." The 9th house rules religious observance and philosophical attitudes, while the 3rd house rules the native's interactions with those close to him -- brothers, neighbors, etc.

96. The authorities previously cited do not mention a Part of Law, but perhaps this is another name for the "Part of Religion" or "Part of Faith." See below.

And so, if Mercury is in a domicile of Saturn, or in aspect with it, it signifies that the native will have deep knowledge, and that he will be persistent, and that he will keep his own thoughts hidden. He will hate joy, laughter, and games, and will live in an humble manner and endure restricted means and hard work, especially if the fortunes do not aspect it and if they are cadent.

But if it is in a domicile of Jupiter, or in aspect with it, it signifies that he will have fame, good fortune, and good faith.

And if it is in a domicile of Mars, or in an evil aspect with it, it signifies that the native will have bad faith, be pouring out blood, encountering injuries, and deriding his own law. But if it is in a good aspect with it, he will be a beautiful builder of [the sort of] lies that were never previously contrived by anyone, an inventor of every sort of wickedness and of new and outrageous crimes, a decorator of falsity, a finger-pointer, and an informer.

And if it is in the domicile of the Sun, or in aspect with it, he will be serious, humble, trustworthy, and wise, skilled in books and judgments, religious, and loving riches.

But if it is in a domicile of Venus, or in aspect with it, he will be generous, good-spirited, and very joyful. And if Mars aspects it, he will be unconcerned and a scoffer at his own law.

But if it is in the domicile of the Moon, or in aspect with it, it signifies that the native will fear God and delight in the good reputation that he will attain, [and that he will be] famous and praiseworthy.

And if Mercury is in its own domicile, it signifies that the native will be a master of knowledge and of good faith, wise in divine books, and in books of other sorts, from which he will attain fame and a celebrated reputation, especially if Jupiter aspects it.

And if the 9th sign is common, and its lord is in a common sign, it signifies that the native will be unstable in his faith, especially if Mars aspects the 9th. But if the 9th is a mobile sign, it signifies that the native will have his doubts about faith or law, and that he will change from one to another, and that he will not be constant in any one thing. But if the 9th sign is fixed, and its lord is placed in a fixed sign, it signifies his constancy in faith, counsel, and action, especially if Mars does not impedite it.

And if the [planet] that has the principal dignities in the 9th house [is posited] either in the ASC [or] in the MC, free from [any aspect of] the evil [planets] (for the lord of the 9th house is fortunately placed in these houses), pronounce freely that the native will display good sense in the best things, be a lover of wisdom and the arts,[97] and perfect in his faith, especially if Jupiter is lord of the 9th or aspects the lord of its sign.

---

97. That is, in various "arts & crafts" and fields of knowledge, not necessarily in the fine arts.

And know that when the lord of the 9th is oriental in those houses
that we have mentioned, the native will disclose his own law; but if
it is occidental, he will hide and conceal his own law. When Mercury
is with the Moon in the 9th sign, in his own domicile or in the
Moon's domicile, and the Part of Faith⁹⁸ is with them, it signifies
that the native will be subtle in knowledge and wisdom, and he will
be an expositor of books, dreams, and judgments, or he will be a
prophet. And if Jupiter is with them or aspects them, it signifies
that he will be truthful, [well-]received by all men, good,
benevolent, and beloved by men, and a searcher for insights into
great and serious matters.

When the Head of the Dragon of the Moon is in the 3rd house in
nocturnal nativities, it signifies that the native will be well-known
and firm in the law and in his own faith. Especially if the Sun or
Jupiter or Mercury aspect it, or if two of them aspect it, because
then he will be generally better and more praised. And if the 9th
house is a domicile of Jupiter and the Moon is in it in nocturnal
nativities, it signifies that the native will be a skilled astronomer
and an annunciator of divinations and things that will happen in the
future.⁹⁹ Similarly, if Mercury is lord of the 9th, or there is in
the 9th a star of the nature of Mercury.

Furthermore, when you find the Moon in the ASC, it signifies that
the native will be an unpleasant sort [of person] and evil-minded.
Similarly, if the Part of Fortune is in the ASC or the Angle of Earth
in diurnal and nocturnal nativities, it signifies that the native
will be an unpleasant sort and one doing evil to those close to him.

Also, when the Part of Faith is with Saturn, it signifies that the
native will be one who is continually searching into things and
putting them off. And if it is with Jupiter, it signifies that the
native will be of good faith and that he will have a beautiful manner
of speech. And if it is with Mars, he will be of bad faith and evil
habits. But if it is with the Sun, and yet not under the Sun beams,
the native will be wise, enjoying a name and good repute. And if it
is with Venus, it signifies that he will be benevolent and a lover of
play and joy. And if it is with Mercury, it signifies knowledge of
arithmetic,¹⁰⁰ books, and business. And if it is with the Moon, it
signifies that the native will be generous and neat.

And if the 9th house is a domicile of Jupiter, or the exaltation
of the Sun, the Moon, or Venus, and the lord of its own exaltation is
the lord of the triplicity of the luminary that has the dignity,¹⁰¹
and it is in a good place in the circle, the native will get his

----

98. This Part seems to have various names. Abu Ma'shar (*Great Introduction*, viii. 4, "The Parts
of the Twelve Houses") calls the third Part of the 9th house the Part of Religion and gives the
formula: Mercury - Moon + ASC by day, and Moon - Mercury + ASC by night. Al-Biruni calls it the
Fate of Timidity and Hiding. Ibn Ezra calls it the Fate of Modesty. Leopold calls it the Part of
Faith & Religion. Guido Bonatti (*Ten Treatises on Astrology*, viii.2, 12) agrees with Abu Ma'shar.
99. The printed text mistakenly ends the current paragraph at this point.
100. The reader should bear in mind that the author lived in the 9th century.
101. Bonatti (loc. cit.) explains this awkward sentence: "If the 9th house is Aries, Cancer, or
Pisces, and the Sun, the Moon, or Jupiter [respectively] is lord of the triplicity of the Light of
Time..."

livelihood from faith or from law. And he will be of good faith, praised and beloved by men. And if any one of the fortunes is in the 3rd sign or the 9th, the native will be fortunate through faith, the law, or the various branches of knowledge. Similarly, if the lords of these two houses are in good places in the circle, free from [any aspect of] the evil [planets], it signifies the same thing. But if Saturn is lord of the 9th sign, it signifies that the native will be wise, especially if it is in aspect with the fortunes, and not retrograde, nor under the Sun beams. For this planet, when it is under the Sun beams, signifies deception and concealment, but when retrograde, lies.

And look at the signs of the 3rd and the 9th house and their lords, and the Part of Faith and its lord. And if they are satisfactorily placed, all or most of them free from impediment and from falling from the angles,[102] the native will be of good faith and religion. But if they are impedited, or if evil [planets] are in the 3rd or the 9th house, or they are in square or opposition aspect to [either of these houses], it signifies an evil and corrupted faith. The Moon too, if it is lord of the 3rd, or the lord of the 3rd is in the 9th, or vice versa the lord of the 9th is in the 3rd, or she herself or Mercury is in them, and Jupiter or Venus are lords of the houses and posited in angles, it signifies a kingdom and elevation [of the native] because of things related to faith.

And if you want to know in which age the native will have the best faith, take [as principal significators] the lords of the triplicity of the Part of Faith, because whichever one of them is the best by condition and house, and fortunately placed in the 3rd [house] from the Sun, in the time of that one the native will have the best faith and [observation of] religion.

Chapt. 30. *The Native's Dignity and Work, and the Things Signified by the Tenth House.*

Look at the 10th sign and its lord, and the Part of Kingdom[103] with its lord, and the Sun in diurnal nativities, or the Moon in nocturnal nativities. And you should know which of them has the most dignities, because if there is *Alictisal*[104] between the one that has the most dignities and the lord of the ASC, or a conjunction or configuration, the native will be a royal person, and he will grow rich from his kingdom, and he will attain the greatest honor.

But if there is no *Alictisal* between them, nor a conjunction, nor a configuration [of any sort], the native will be unknown to the king, [a person] of moderate worth, and little power. But if the planet among these that has the greatest dignity is in its own domicile and in good aspect with the lord of the ASC, the native will

---

102. That is, they are not cadent.
103. The identity of this Part is uncertain. Abu Ma'shar (loc. cit.) gives the formula: the Moon - Mars + ASC by day, and Mars - Moon + ASC by night. Al-Biruni calls it the Part of Kings and Sultans. Ibn Ezra calls it the Fate of Royalty. Leopold calls it the Part of the King. Bonatti (op. cit., viii.2, 13) agrees with Abu Ma'shar.
104. See the note to Chapt. 15 above for an explanation of this technical term.

have a kingdom and great power. And if there is no aspect between them, the native will have only meager power and [be distantly related] to kings.

Chapt. 31. *The Native's Place in the Kingdom.*

In the matter of the kingdom, look at the lord of the ASC and the lord of the MC. If there is an application between them, it signifies that the native will gain a name and advantage from kings. But if the lord of the ASC applies to the lord of the 10th house, the native will certainly gain advantages from kings, but through his own inquiry and petition. But if the lord of the MC applies to the lord of the ASC, it is a sign that kings and princes will summon him unasked and raise him up. And if this application happens in angles,[105] it will be [to] A dignity, by means of which he will attain great power and a great name, and especially if it is in the ASC or in the MC. But if the lord of the ASC is in an angle and the lord of the MC is cadent, it signifies that the kingdom will be an important one and that the native's name will be great, but his acts will be unimportant and unnoticed. But if the lord of the 10th is in an angle and the lord of the ASC is cadent, the native will be outstanding in his actions, but [personally] inglorious and low-born. And if both are cadent, it signifies the low quality of both the native and his actions.

When the lord of the ASC is in the MC, it signifies that the native will be a member of the royal court and involved in work for the king. And if there is a good aspect between them,[106] it signifies friendship between the king and the native; but if it is a bad aspect, enmity and trouble. But if there is no application between the lord of the ASC and the lord of the MC, look at the application between the lord of the ASC and the Sun, because if the lord of the ASC applies to the Sun and the Sun to the lord of the ASC, it signifies that the native will profit from the king and will be conjoined to kings and nobles, especially if the application is from good houses. And if the application is by square or opposition, it signifies that he will mingle with kings and will be involved in their business affairs and will acquire assets from them, but he will be aggravated by the kings. And if the application is by trine or sextile aspect, it promises the native the love of the king, and the acquisition of money and honor. But if the lord of the ASC is conjunct the Sun, it signifies that the native will be a familiar and faithful [supporter] of the king, and one who knows his secrets, and he will have honor through fire,[107] and the king will attach himself to him, and he will be gracious in his words when he is with him. If the lord of the ASC is one of the superior planets, and it is in the MC applied to its lord, it signifies that he will be conjoined with nobles as well as with kings, and he will be like one of them, and he will have business with all of them. And if one of the inferior planets is lord of the ASC, and it is posited in the MC, or the lord of the MC is applied to it, it signifies that he will hold some

---

105. In the printed Latin text the comma before *applicatio* should be after it.
106. That is, between the lord of the ASC and the lord of the MC.
107. What this means is uncertain.

office of the king or of some major domo of his. And if the lord of
the ASC is applied to one of the luminaries, or contrariwise, it
signifies the conjunction of the native with kings. And if it is
received, he will derive benefit from this; but if it is not
received, little advantage will come back to the native from that
source.

Surely domicile is privileged over
exaltation?

Chapt. 32. *The Native's Prosperity and Power.*

To investigate the native's power and his kingdom, consider the
planet that has an application to the lord of the ASC, or
contrariwise, to which the lord of the ASC applies. If it is in its
own exaltation, it signifies the conjunction of the native with kings
and nobles. And if it is in its own domicile, it signifies his
conjunction with [persons of] lesser [degree] than these, but still
high[-born] and noble. And in the case of the term or triplicity, say
[that they are still less] so, because they themselves are less
[powerful] than domicile or exaltation. After this, look at the Part
of Work[108] and its lord. If it is in a house that harmonizes with the
ASC, free from [any aspect with] the evil [planets], or the lord of
the ASC and the lord of the Part in angles, it signifies that the
native will have much work and little quiet. And if the lord of the
Part applies to a planet that is in its own exaltation, it signifies
the elevation of the native's status and the greatness of his power,
especially if the star is in an angle. And if it is placed in its own
domicile, he will be somewhat less; and if in term or triplicity,
still less than that; but if in face, he will be below that which I
have said. And if the planet is increased in course, it signifies
much idleness and that the native will love solitary places,
according to the nature of the sign in which it is.

Chapt. 33. *The Native's Profession.*

Begin with the value and rank of the native's work and profession,
which is ascertained from the nature, condition, quality, and
strength of that planet which has the principal testimony in the
significations of these things. Know, therefore, that the
significator of profession is[109] that planet which is in the ASC or
the MC, oriental from the Sun and occidental from the Moon. Also, in
diurnal nativities, the one to which the Moon [first] applies after
the New Moon or Full Moon preceding the nativity, and the Part of
Fortune in nocturnal nativities, and the planet to which the Moon
applies in the hour of the nativity.

Moreover, the planets that signify professions by their own nature
are Mars, Venus, and Mercury. If you find one of them in the ASC or
the MC, oriental and having some dignity there, and in good aspect
with the Sun or the Moon, it signifies that the profession will be

---

108. Abu Ma'shar has a Part of Work and of the Thing which must be done, for which he gives the
formula: Jupiter - Sun + ASC by day, and Sun - Jupiter + ASC by night. Al-Biruni calls it the Part
of Operations and Orders in Medical Treatment. Ibn Ezra calls it the Fate of the Task which is to
be Accomplished. Leopold and Bonatti agree with Abu Ma'shar.

109. The printed text has 'and' instead of 'is', as noted in the Errata.

prestigious, useful, and honorable according to the nature of the
planet that signifies this. But if none of these three is in the ASC
or the MC, and one of them is in the Angle of Earth or in the 7th,
the profession will be something less than what I have said, with
alternating periods of hard work and idleness.

But if none of those [are found] as I have said, make your
testimony on the native's profession from the lord of the 10th house
if the nativity is diurnal or from that planet to which the Moon
applies if the nativity is nocturnal, especially if it has dignity in
the house of the Part of Fortune. For that one which has the
strongest testimony and is in the strongest house will be the
significator of the native's profession. If it good by nature and in
a good house, and Mercury aspects it with a fortunate aspect, it
signifies that the native will have a good profession and riches, and
he will profit from his business activities and from his knowledge of
writing and arithmetic, giving much, and receiving much, and endowed
with good abilities and proper character.

And if Saturn aspects it with friendly rays, it signifies that the
native will get his living from cultivation of the earth and from
planting trees;[110] and he will be the eldest of his own house and the
one in command. And if Jupiter aspects it, the native will be a
writer and an orator, honored among kings and nobles. And if Mars
aspects it with a fortunate aspect, he will be a physician, or a
prophet, or a necromancer, clever, and prudent in his own work. And
if the Sun aspects it, or is with it so that it does [not][111] burn it
up with its own rays, it signifies that he will be a high magistrate,
and a person of the highest station, and a secretary of kings, of the
highest worth among them, of a noble profession, and of much
learning. And if the Moon aspects it, it signifies knowledge,
learning, good fortune, and progress[112] for the native. And if Venus
aspects it, it signifies that the native will be connected with the
women of kings and nobles, and much valued by them, and that he will
gain advantage from them.[113] And if any one of the evil [planets]
aspects it, and is in a strong house in [one of] its dignities, it
signifies hard work and difficulty in connection with the profession.
And know that in that year in which the profection of the ASC comes
by rays to the sign of the MC, if there is in it any one of the
planets signifying the profession, the native will renew his
profession according to the nature of the substance of the planet
which is there and according to its configuration with the other
stars.

---

110. The printed text has ...ex cultu terrarum, & populatione earum... 'from the cultivation of
lands and from their population'. The second phrase doesn't make much sense. In Guido Bonatti (Ten
Treatises on Astrology, ix.3, "The 10th House", Chapt. 1) we find ...in cultu terrarum arborumque
plantatione... 'in cultivation of the earth and planting trees'. I conjecture Abu 'Ali's text
should read ...in cultu terrarum et plantatione arborum... with the translation as given above.

111. Adds Bonatti (loc. cit.).

112. The printed text has perfectionem 'perfection' and Bonatti (loc. cit.) has
perfectamque...fortunam 'and completely good fortune'. But I think both printed texts are wrong and
the correct reading is profectum 'progress' or 'advancement'.

113. He might, for example, be a merchant supplying food delicacies or jewelry or fine clothing
to the wives of the rich and powerful.

Chapt. 34. *The Native's Audacity and Courage.*

Look at the Part of Audacity[114] and its lord, in which places of the circle they are, and the planets, either fortunes or evil [planets] aspecting them. And if they are in angles, and especially if they are in a domicile of Mars or the Sun or Jupiter, with an aspect from one of them, or if the Moon is in an angle with the Sun or Mars, or if the Sun and the Moon along with Mars aspect the Part and its lord by trine radiation, it signifies that the native will be a man of action. And if the Part of Fortune is with Mars and Jupiter, it signifies that the native will be audacious and the leader of an army. And if one of the luminaries is in the ASC and the other is in the MC, it signifies that the native will be audacious, and a governor, and leader of an army, and bold in the shedding of blood.

And if the ASC is a masculine sign, and the luminaries and the lord of the ASC are in masculine signs, while Mars is dwelling in an angle, it signifies that the native will be audacious and that his commands will be carried out, and he will love the shedding of blood, especially if the Part of Audacity is with Mars or Mars is lord of the Part. And when the lord of the Part of Audacity is with Mars in the 9th house, it signifies that the native will be stupid and of little piety. And a greater good, by which the native is made fortunate in the matter of action is when Jupiter aspects Mars with a good aspect. And if, with this aspect between them, there is reception, the native will be a model of action. When the Part of Audacity is with Saturn or in evil aspect with it, it signifies that there will be hypocrisy in the native's action, and he will be weak in it.

And when Mars is in a water sign, it signifies weakness in action. But there will be great audacity when Mars is in any one of the angles, and especially in Aries or in its triplicity. And when it is in the first [angle], it signifies that the native will shun men, and he will desire slaughter and the outpouring of human blood. The same thing will be [signified] when Mars is in the domicile of the Moon. And when Mars is with Mercury in an angle under the Sun beams, it signifies that the native will be a public bandit and an infester of highways, and he will be known throughout the land because of this. Moreover, when Mars is with the Moon in an angle under the Sun beams, it signifies that the native will be a secret thief, and a perforator,[115] and a thief in the night. And when Mars is not in an angle, it signifies that the native will not be famous or honored for his action. And when the Part of Military Service[116] is not in a domicile of Mars, the native will not be honored in the military for his courage. But always, when the star of Mars is in the rising sign, it signifies a vicious and unscrupulous man, who will engage in

---

114. I suppose he means the Part of Boldness, which is one of the six ancient Parts associated with the Part of Fortune. Paul of Alexandria (*Introduction to Astrology*, Chapt. 23) gives the formula: Fortuna - Mars + ASC by day, and Mars - Fortuna + ASC by night.

115. Presumably, a thief who bores through walls to gain entry to a house or shop.

116. This is perhaps the Part that is calculated by the formula: Saturn - Mars + ASC by day, and Mars - Saturn + ASC by night. Al-Biruni calls it the Part of Armies and Police. Leopold calls it the Part of Soldiers and Ministers.

shameful and lustful acts and perpetrate offenses of every kind. And
answer this way [too] in interrogations.

Chapt. 35. *Friends.*

Decide the condition of friends from the 11th house and its lord,
and from the planets that you find in it, and from Venus, and from
the Part of Friends.[117] If most of these are fortunes, it signifies
that the native will have many friends and companions, and especially
if there is an application between the lord of the 11th and the lord
of the ASC. And if you find fortunes in the 11th sign, or in square
or opposite aspect to it, it signifies that the native will have many
friends and associates, and that they will be fortunate. And if you
find evil [planets] in it, or in square or opposite aspect to it, it
signifies few friends and associates and that their assets will be
scanty.

And if the planet that has the most dignities in the house of
friends is Saturn, it signifies that most of his friends will be old
men, slaves, and captives. But if it is Jupiter, many of them will be
nobles and rich people of great worth and repute. And if it is Mars,
most of them will be [military] leaders and princes and warlike men.
But if it is the Sun, most of them will be [military] leaders and
princes, kings, and nobles. But if [it is] Venus, they will be women
and effeminate men. But if it is Mercury, they will mostly be writers
and businessmen and wise men and artisans. But if it is the Moon,
most of his friends will be nobles, but many [others] will be
commoners. And so every star signifies according to its own nature;
and according to   its strength   and fortunate   or unfortunate
[condition], the native will have advantage or disadvantage.

Besides all this, look at the lord of the ASC and the lord of the
11th, and the application that is between them and their mutual
reception, and how much one of them makes the other fortunate or
unfortunate, and their places in the circle. For if they are in
mobile signs, it signifies that the native's friends will seldom be
constant in their attitude towards him. But if [they are] in common
signs, it indicates that sometimes there will be friendship and at
other times it will break up. But if they are both in fixed signs, it
signifies firm and lasting friendship of the friends towards the
native.

But where the lord of the ASC impedites the lord of the 11th, the
friends will suffer some impediment from the native. But if the lord
of the 11th impedites the lord of the ASC, the native will receive
some harm from his friends. And if each of them makes the other
fortunate, the friends and the native will have mutual good and
benefit among themselves. But if the lord of the 11th does not aspect

---

117. Abu Ma'shar, Al-Biruni, Leopold, and Guido Bonatti give the formula: Mercury - Moon + ASC
by day and by night. (Ibn Ezra gets it backwards by mistake.) This Part also appears in the list
given in the oldest MS of Heliodorus's *Commentary on Paul,* but it says to reverse it by night.
However, the same MS in a different place contains a scholium on Hephaestio of Thebes which says
that in the 4th book [of the *Pentateuch*] of Dorotheus he takes the Lot of Friendship with the same
formula, but 'by day and by night', which agrees with Abu Ma'shar.

his own house and Venus does not aspect the lord of her domicile, and the lord of the Part of Friends [does] not [aspect] the Part, it signifies that the native will be odious to men, nor will he delight in their company, being a lover of solitude. But when the house of friends is made fortunate and is essentially good, it signifies good circumstances and good fortune for the friends. [But] if it is made unfortunate, conversely it threatens them with bad luck and poverty.

Chapt. 36. *Enemies, and the Things Signified by the Twelfth House.*

For things concerning enemies, look at the 12th sign and its lord, and at the planet located in the 12th house, and at the Part of Enemies[118] and its lord, and at Saturn. For if the strongest of these is an evil [planet] or impedited, and it aspects the lord of the ASC, it signifies that the native will have many enemies and harm from them.

But if the one that has the most dignities is a fortune or is made fortunate, and if it aspects the lord of the ASC, it signifies that the native will have few enemies and that he will have a good name among men. Similarly, if the lord of the 12th does not aspect the lord of the ASC, it signifies that the native will have few enemies. When the lord of the 12th and the lord of the ASC are in mutual good aspect with each other, it signifies little or no harm from enemies. Similarly, when one of the two fortunes is in the house of enemies and has some dignity there, it signifies that his adversaries will be good men who will not harm him. But if there is an infortune there, it signifies harm to the enemies [themselves]. And if the lord of the 12th is in an angle or in a succedent and it has any dignity there, it signifies that the enemies will be noble and strong. But if it is cadent and peregrine, or under the Sun beams, or in its own fall, it signifies want and bad circumstances for the [native's] enemies. For when any one of the evil [planets] is located in the house of enemies, or when the lord of the house of enemies is made unfortunate by any one of the evil [planets], and from evil houses, it signifies that the native will have good luck against his enemies, and it shows that they will have adversity. But if any one of the fortunes is there, or the lord of the 12th applies to any of them, it signifies strength, and good luck, and victory for the enemies against the native. And if the lord of the 12th is in opposition to the Sun or the Moon, or is [posited] in the ASC, it signifies many enemies and persons attacking the native. But if it is an evil [planet], there will be enmity in commonplace things. But if [it is] a fortune, there will be enmity over great and lofty things.

---

118. Abu Ma'shar has a Part of Enemies "according to some of the Ancients," for which the formula is: Mars - Saturn + ASC by day and by night. Al-Biruni agrees exactly. Guido Bonatti calls it the Part of Secret Enemies. Leopold calls it the Part of Enemies. These authors also have a Part of Enemies "according to Hermes," for which the formula is: Cusp of the 12th House - Lord of the 12th + ASC by day and by night. (Ibn Ezra gets them mixed up and says the Mars/Saturn one is due to Hermes and that it should be reversed at night.)

Chapt. 37. *The Quality of Death and its Occasions.*

For the causes and occasions of death, look at the ASC and its
lord, and the Part of Death[119] and its lord, and the 4th sign with
its lord, and the good or evil planets that are in this house, and
those that aspect it, and the lord of the triplicity of the Angle of
Earth, and the lord of the 7th house, and the 8th sign from the Sun
and the Moon and their lords, because if one or more of these has
more powerful dignities, is in [one of] the aforesaid houses, safe
from any impediments by the evil [planets], from retrogradation, and
from combustion, and the 8th house is safe -- that is, none of the
infortunes is in it or in opposition to it, it signifies the
liberation of the native [from the possibility of a bad death] and
the goodness of his death.

And if the Almuten over these places is impedited and retrograde
or combust or in its own fall, it signifies a bad and foreign death,
and every star has its own special signification in this matter. For
if Saturn is most dignified in these places, or its rays or its
disposition is found there, and it is not impedited, it signifies
death with pains and long-lasting tortures from cold and wetness. And
if it is impedited, it signifies death in the snow or through
submersion in water.

But if Jupiter is more dignified than the rest [of the planets],
and it is safe from impediments, the native's death will be from
pains in the lungs or from spitting up blood or from pain in the
stomach or from a liver ailment or from drinking [too much] wine. But
if it is impedited, the native's death will occur through the agency
of a king, or a king's order, or through [some action of the] people.

But if Mars is the most dignified of these and not impedited, his
death will be sudden from some hot sickness and from blood or from
some sort of acute and intensive[120] ailment. But if it is impedited,
his death will be through the agency of fire or iron, either in an
altercation or a murder.

And if the Sun is more dignified, or its rays or its disposition
is the strongest, and it is not impedited, death will come to the
native from some burning ailment among slaves, relations, or his own
family, among his own people. But if it is impedited, death will come
to him in some way through his parents, or kings, or relations, or
from an ailment of the stomach or the mouth. And he will die amidst
an assembly or crowd of people, or among a crowd of bathers, or the
king will order his death.

But if Venus is the most dignified by its rays or by its
disposition, and it is not impedited, death will come to him from
some belly ailment or from hemorrhoids. But if it is impedited, it
signifies death from sexual license[121] or poisoned medicines.

----

119. Abu Ma'shar, Al-Biruni, Ibn Ezra, and Leopold give the formula: Cusp of the 8th House -
Moon + Saturn by day and by night.
120. Reading *intensivo* 'intensive' in place of *incentivo* 'leading?'.
121. That is, from some disease contracted through indulgence in promiscuous sex.

And if Mercury is the most dignified by its rays or its disposition, and it is not impeded, his death will be from madness, or red cholera, or from various pains in the intestines, or from jaundice. But if it is impeded, the cause of death will be from his handling of writing, from some speech or counsel that he is going to give.

And when the Moon is the most dignified and not impeded, death will come to him from various [causes] arising from wet food, from drink, and from sexual license. And if she is impeded, the native's death will be according to the nature of the planet impediting the Moon.

Moreover, when the planets annnouncing death are in their own domiciles or their own exaltations and free from impediments, his death will be on his own grounds and in his own house -- in better and nicer circumstances. But if they are impeded and outside of their own domiciles and exaltations, his death will occur while he is traveling in some foreign region. But if they are cadent, his death will be due to a fall from a high place. If [they are] in their falls, his death will occur in pits or waters or in ruined places. And if they are retrograde, his death will be from suffocation or being crushed in a mob.

For when the Moon in nocturnal nativities or the Sun in diurnal nativities is conjoined to the evil [planets], or in evil aspect with them, it signifies a bad death for the native and difficulty in dying. And if the Moon is conjunct the Sun, or in square or opposition aspect [to it], his death will be by fire. And if Mars is in the 4th sign impediting the lord of the 8th, his death will be by iron. But if Saturn is there impediting the lord of the 8th or in the 4th sign from the Sun or from the Moon, death will come to him from torture or prison. And if Mars is with the Head of the Dragon of the Moon in the 4th sign, his death will be on a cross, or he will be hung. But if Mercury is with the Tail in the 4th sign, death will come to him from plots, or through some scheme, or through poison or necromancy. And if the Moon is with the Tail there, his death will be from poison or from medicines taken as a purge.

If the first lord of the triplicity of the Angle of Earth, or the setting degree, or its lord, and the Sun in diurnal nativities, or the Moon in nocturnal nativities, is impeded, the native will end his life with a bad death or one in a foreign place. But if the significators of death are impedited above the earth, his death will be manifest and talked about or famous. But if they are impedited under the earth, his death will be hidden, and if the significators of death are in earth signs, his death will be in a cavern or underneath some ruin. And if they are in air signs, the native's death will be on the back of an animal, or by the hands of man in the high places of earth, on a cross, or something else [elevated]. But if they are in fire signs, death will come to him through fire or through the pervasive heat of the air. And if the significators are in water signs, his death will be from wet things: from snow, water, and such like.

But if there is a fortune in the 8th and the 8th house is made fortunate, or [the fortune] is applying to the lord of the 8th, [or] similarly when any [planet] is made fortunate in the Angle of Earth or is with its lord, it signifies a good death. And if there is an infortune in the 8th, or with the lord of the 8th, his death will be stinking and disgraceful. Similarly, when there is an infortune in the 4th, or applying to the lord of the 4th sign, it threatens death in outlying regions. But if this infortune is Mars, he will die through iron or through fire. But if it is Saturn, he will die on account of poison or [bad] food or some drug.

Chapt. 38. *The General Way or Method of Judgment of the Twelve Houses of Heaven.*

The general way in which you ought to look for the judgments of the twelve houses is just as I shall now show you, if God is willing.

Look first at the individual houses and observe carefully which of the fortunes or the evil [planets] is in them, or aspects them by square or opposition aspect, and how the lord of that house is situated whose significations you seek, and in which house of the circle it is located, and the configuration of it with the [other] planets, and the circumstances of the Part that refers to that house, and its house. Also, look at the condition and quality of its lord, and its place in the circle, and the configuration of the [other] planets with it. Look also at the condition of the significators -- if they are oriental or occidental, direct or retrograde, and with whom they are configured, fortunes or infortunes, and if they are in angles, succedents, or cadents.

For if most of the significators of any particular house, or the strongest one of them, are made fortunate, and free from [any aspect of] the evil [planets], and free from impediment, it signifies good fortune in the nature of the thing signified by that house, and especially if a fortune by its configuration in good houses of the circle has also contributed to strengthening and augmenting [the house] by means of its testimony. But if you find the significators of any thing configured with the evil [planets], or retrograde, or combust, or in their own falls, viz. falling from their own exaltations and from the angles, or in their detriments, it signifies misfortune in the thing signified, and especially if cadent and posited in inauspicious houses, as we have said, they are also conjoined to the infortunes, or in square or opposition to them.

And if there is any one of these things concerning which it may be necessary to know [how] much or [how] little, [or whether there will be] an increase or a decrease, say about this in accordance with the [situation] in which you have found the significators in their own houses and according to what their position is in signs or in houses signifying much or little.

Chapt. 39. *Saturn in Its Own Domicile and in Those of the Other Planets in Diurnal and Nocturnal Nativities.*

When Saturn is in his own domicile in diurnal nativities, it signifies friendship with noble and magnates, and accumulation of property, especially if it is in the ASC or with the Part of Fortune. And if the nativity is nocturnal, [Saturn] in its own house, signifies hard work and a long stretch of it and much sickness.

And if it is in a domicile of Jupiter in diurnal nativities, it signifies beauty, and an abundance of riches, and truth. But if the nativity is nocturnal, he will be an arranger of things for kings and magnates, and his father may be killed.

And when it is in a domicile of Mars, he will have a heart like a stone, little pity, and a lot of anger in situations where he ought not to [allow himself to] get angry. And he will not gain advancement because of good things [that he has done], but he will prosper more in evil.

The same Saturn in diurnal nativities located in the domicile of the Sun declares good fortune for the native and good circumstances for his father and augmentation of [the native's] assets. And if it is a nocturnal birth, it signifies the affliction of illness for the native and his father.

But if you discover it in a domicile of Venus, it denotes his passion for poor women, and those hampered by infirmity, and for common, worthless [women].

And when this same [planet] is in a domicile of Mercury, it signifies that the native will be thrifty and that he will preserve and investigate the different branches of learning and the secrets in hidden books, on which account he will suffer harm. And he will have an impediment and slowness of the tongue. He will have a very bad mental attitude, and men will hate him and say that he has done things that he hasn't done.

If you find this same [planet] in the domicile of the Moon, do not doubt that it signifies infirmity for the native and many maladies for his mother; also, it will destroy his mother's estate during her lifetime.

Chapt. 40. *Jupiter in Its Own Domicile and in Those of the Other Planets.*

When you find Jupiter in a domicile of Saturn, it denotes seriousness and narrowness of heart and much wealth,[122] but commonly he will represent himself as poor, and he will be weak-hearted, slow-acting, thinking evil every day, and persevering in it. And he will act in secret. And evil will come to him from various directions.

---

122. The printed text has *luctus* 'mourning', but this is inconsistent with the next phrase. Leopold (op. cit., Treatise VII, at the end) summarizes Abu 'Ali's Planets in Signs and Planets in Houses. At this point he has *lucri* 'wealth', which must be correct.

But if it is in its own domicile in a diurnal nativity, he will be fortunate and rich, beloved also and powerful among kings and princes. But if the birth is nocturnal, he will be the contrary of what we have said. For he will be obliged to acquire his living daily, and he will say those things that are not and never were, and he will have connection with religious men, or he will be a leader in law or religion.

When this same [planet] is located in a domicile of Mars, he will be praised for all his actions,[123] will have continuous good fortune, and have familarity with kings, princes, and [military] leaders. And if Jupiter is in an angle or a succedent of an angle in a masculine sign, he will be a prince and the leader of an army, and [a man] of great worth and a very famous name.

But if this same [planet] is in the domicile of the Sun, he will be handsome, with good talents, associated with kings, and praised among them and also before the whole population. And if, besides what I have said, it is in an angle or a succedent, free from [any aspect of] the evil [planets] and from impediments, he will have great good fortune and great wealth, and he will be a king or like a king, but especially in a diurnal nativity.

If you see this same [planet] in a domicile of Venus in the nativities of males, it signifies connection with nobles, and joy, and advantage from marriage[124] with noble women. But if the nativity is that of a woman, she will acquire benefit from captivity and advancement because of faith and religion.

When the same [planet] is in a domicile of Mercury, the native will be a businessman, rich, giving much, and receiving much from his business operations, and praised, and he will have dominion over some men in secret, and he will get money from this, and he will be praised with the highest praises.

And if this same [planet] appears in the domicile of the Moon in diurnal nativities, and especially [if it is] in an angle or a succedent, he will be fortunate and [possessed] of much wealth and great authority, connected with kings and nobles. But if the nativity is nocturnal, he will be a leading figure in law, [a person] of good talent in his arts, and famous because of them.

Chapt. 41. *Mars in Its Own Domicile and in Those of the Other Planets.*

When Mars is in a domicile of Saturn, the native will be bold, a devil, carrying to completion everything he starts, but he will squander the resources of his own parents, and he will see the death of his own elder brothers.

---

123. The printed text has *artibus* 'arts', but *actibus* 'actions' seems more appropriate (Leopold omits the whole phrase). But compare Jupiter in Cancer below.

124. The printed text has *desponsatione* 'marriage'. Leopold has *dispensatione* 'stewardship', which I think is a false reading. Guido Bonatti, who paraphrases Abu ʿAli's text towards the end of his *Treatise on Nativities*, has *matrimonium consum(m)abit cum eis* 'he will marry them'.

With this same [planet] in a domicile of Jupiter, the native will be noble, honored, and handsome, a friend of nobles and magnates. And if Jupiter in turn is in a domicile of Mars in a good configuration, the native will be like a leader of armies, conquering his adversaries.

But if [Mars] is in its own domicile, he will be famous, honored, and rich, and very talented and learned, skilled in geometry; and he will have good success in everything he does, especially if the nativity is nocturnal. But if it happens to be diurnal, and [Mars] is in Aries, with no aspect from the fortunes, he will be ill-natured, inflicting injuries on everyone, and he will have hidden pains and a fall from a high place. And if it is in Scorpio, everything we have just said is reduced in magnitude.

If [Mars] is in the domicile of the Sun, it signifies the death of the native from some infirmity that he will have in his belly, and particularly in the stomach, [or] in the eyes; and he will work at those things that are important for working with fire.[125] And his death will be sudden, or he will be captured, or he will be murdered, or he or his father will die while traveling.

When this same [planet] is in a domicile of Venus, the native will be sexually promiscuous, a fornicator, performing sinful acts with the wives of his own kindred, or with his own kinswomen, or he will marry a woman with whom he has previously committed adultery, and he will suffer harm from women. But if it is in Libra, he will suffer harm from fire and iron in hidden places of his body. But if it is in Taurus, it signifies every kind of lewdness combined with malice.

If you find this same [planet] in a domicile of Mercury, it signifies that the native will have [superior] understanding and very great talent, and he will be clever and bold, and he will experience poverty. And greater profit will come to him from theft and robbery, or [else] he will be wise, a teacher of languages, or the pupil of a writer, who writes false documents, and he will excel his comrades in knowledge and talent.

But with this same [planet] in the domicile of the Moon, he will be light in motion, agile, a careful investigator of the branches of knowledge and of profound statements, and he will be bold in carrying out bad works. And he will suffer some hurt or some impediment in his belly or in hidden parts of his body. And his mother will have a long illness, and her death will be sudden, and the native will squander her estate.

Chapt. 42. *The Sun in Its Own Domicile and in the Domiciles of the Other Planets.*

When the Sun, especially in a diurnal nativity, is in a domicile of Saturn, he will be closemouthed, laughing, a deceiver, successful in all his undertakings, and, if it is a nocturnal [nativity], he

---

125. Leopold mentions 'iron' instead of 'fire', and Bonatti mentions both.

will get angry[126] quickly, he will be inconstant in his own things, despising all things, and [a man] of incessant change.

But if [the Sun] is in a domicile of Jupiter, he will be skilled in the cause of his own law, good, not sluggish, and greater than all his own people. But if the nativity is nocturnal, it signifies good rearing and connection with nobles; besides which, he will be a fornicator, engaging in iniquity with the wife of his own father or the wife of some other one of his close relatives.

The same [planet] being in a domicile of Mars, signifies infirmities for the father and the native, but in the nature of the relationships,[127] and it signifies a pain in the liver, but his father will be overcome by the worst kind of death. If it is in Scorpio in diurnal nativities of males, it portends good fortune and elevation for them throughout their whole lives. But if it is in nocturnal nativities, it takes away somewhat from this good fortune.

When the same [planet is] in its own domicile in diurnal nativities in an angle or in the succedent of an angle, he will be beloved, ruling, rich, great, and strong, and riches will come to him from highly-placed men, and from leasing lands, and from managing country estates. But in nocturnal nativities, it signifies that his father will have little talent, and he will be an orphan, and he will be captured while traveling, and it may signify that the native will wish to be separated from his parents.

If this same [planet] is in a domicile of Venus, [as] a diviner he will explain dreams, and things concealed will be revealed to him. [He will be] truthful in good, and a [man] of many trips, in which he will greatly delight, but he will live in a shameful and sexually promiscuous manner.[128]

When this same [planet] is in a domicile of Mercury, he will be [a person] of many rumors and of good works, a teacher of the various branches of knowledge, perhaps an astronomer, well-known to all, especially if it is a diurnal nativity. But if it is nocturnal, he will be poor, doing bad things (in fact he will be foul-mouthed in youth), but when he arrives at middle age he will acquire unacknowledged or secret riches. And he will have pains in the stomach or in some hidden part of the body, and he will associate with men who are doing the work of demons.

---

126. The printed text has *nascetur* 'be born' in error for *irascetur* 'get angry' (corrected in the Errata).

127. I don't know what this phrase means, unless it simply refers to the relationship between the positions of the two planets.

128. This whole section is corrupt in the printed text. Leopold, who summarizes, has *expositor somniorum; et investigator absconditorum; et verax et diliget itinera* 'an explainer of dreams; and an investigator of concealed things; and truthful, and he will delight in trips'. Bonatti, who expands, has *significat natum bonum atque veracem somniorum expositorem atque rerum occultarum et etiam absconditarum inventorem extiturum* 'it signifies that the native is a good and truthful explainer of dreams and that he will also be a discoverer of concealed things'. In absence of any further witnesses to the Latin original, the reader can take his choice.

If it is found in the Moon's domicile along with the Tail of the Dragon, Saturn, or Mars, it threatens impediments and dangers to the native's eyes, and it denotes many trips and various dangers in water.

Chapt. 43. *Venus in Its own Domicile and in Those of the Other Planets.*

When Venus is in a domicile of Saturn, the native will have a wife who has been phlebotomized, or he will consort with whores, and he will be criticized for this, and he will be a corrupter of married women, and he will profit from this in his own affairs. But in nocturnal nativities, he will be [a person] of much fornication, and condemned lewdness, and he will have many disputes because of this. And when he enters old age, he will be enriched by the death of his wives.

If this same [planet] is in a domicile of Jupiter, it signifies an increase in the native's dignity, and the acquisition of beautiful clothing, and he will profit in some way from women and through some type of work connected with women, through comrades and relations, and through the wives of nobles, or through some work that he does for them. And his own family will act against him with hatred. But if it is a diurnal nativity, that which I [just] said will occur, but diminished in some way.

When this same [planet] is in a domicile of Mars, the native will suffer misfortune and struggle becaus of women, and he will have to do with slave-girls and bad women....he will get married,[129] and he will fall into arguments and disputes and loss of some kind, and he may even murder his wives because of some suspicions.

But if it is in the domicile of the Sun, the native will be unfortunate because of women, and he will be a lover of girls [so young as to be] almost infants, and he will engage abundantly in sex, and have much desire for it.

The same [planet] found in its own domicile signifies much joy, friendship with women, gladness and delight with other women of his acquaintance; and he[130] will [get to] see what he wants in all his efforts.

And if it is in a domicile of Mercury, he will be connected with the women of men who are religious and reputable, and he will be the master of women's work and of effeminate men, and he will delight in

---

129. The printed text has *malis mulieribus, serviet & consequetur desponsationem* 'bad women, he will serve & he will attain marriage'. Something is obviously wrong. Bonatti expands upon the 'bad women' and goes on to say that the native is very unlikely to marry, but that if he does he will only do so with much difficulty, and that it will cause him trouble subsequently.

130. The printed text seems to be shaky here. Leopold has "...delight with stupid women..." Where "stupid" is Leopold's comment upon the women who have allowed their acquaintance with the native to become too intimate. Perhaps Abu 'Ali means the native will be friendly with some women, and more than friendly with others.

lewdness, and he will make pictures and sculptures and women's
ornaments and such like.

And if it is found in the domicile of the Moon, it signifies
disgraceful lewdness and fickle passions. And in general, when Venus
is in mobile signs, it signifies little stability in any one thing.

Chapt. 44. *Mercury in Its Own Domicile and in Those of the Other Planets.*

When Mercury is in a domicile of Saturn, it indicates seriousness
of tongue and a diversity of words and bad suspicions. And he will
mingle with religious and wise men, and he will be known for
observation of his own law.

If this same [planet] is in a domicile of Jupiter, it portends
connection and friendship with kings and administration of their
affairs and the causes of parties and defenses. And he will be wise
in judgments and in judging.

And when it is in a domicile of Mars, he will make false documents
of deception and lying and cunning, from which he will experience
misfortune.

When the same [planet] is found in the domicile of the Sun, it
signifies an increase in knowledge and memory and investigation of
the profound branches of knowledge.

If you find this same [planet] in a domicile of Venus, it
indicates many friends, and the native will love insolence and
impudence and jokes, and he will fear God, and he will give much and
receive much, and he will do all the things [that require] knowledge,
and he will win over to himself nobles and outstanding men.

But if it is in its own domicile, it signifies all the sciences of
the trivium and quadrivium,[131] and also prophecy, and especially if
it is in Virgo.

But when it is located in the domicile of the Moon, it shows many
trips and honorable inclinations and a good reputation. And he will
be a decent man.

Chapt. 45. *The Moon in Its Own Domicile and in Those of the Other Planets.*

The Moon in a domicile of Saturn indicates sicknesses from [an
excess of] wind. Bad things will be said about him. But if it is
diminished in light, it signifies an infirmity [marked] by a cough
and cold, and pains in the kidneys, especially if it is a nocturnal
nativity. But if it is diurnal, anything of these maladies [that
develops] will be mitigated.

---

131. The so-called "seven liberal arts," consisting of grammar, rhetoric, and logic; and
arithmetic, music, geometry, and astronomy.

If this same [planet] is in a domicile of Jupiter, he will be like a king among his close relations, with much good fame, but he will perform lewd acts with women with whom it is not lawful.

And if it is in a domicile of Mars, he will be [a person] of much anger, bitterness, and contention, and he will mingle with bad men, with robbers and warriors.

This same [planet] in the domicile of the Sun signifies much joy and gladness, friendships with kings, and much fame. The native will experience infirmity in the head and the stomach, especially if [the Moon] is in the beginning or the end of the sign.

But if it is in a domicile of Venus, he will be a lover of women, trying to win them over, and he will have much joy with them and a beautiful life.

This same [planet] located in a domicile of Mercury signifies love for young girls and little girls.

But when it is in its own domicile, the native will have much wealth. He will be [a man] of great authority, connected with kings. But if it is conjoined with or configured with evil [planets], it shows that the native will have various sicknesses and a number of spells of them. But if it is conjoined to the fortunes or is applying to them, it signifies health of body and moderation.

[Latin Editor's Note.]

We found the chapters that follow in another exemplar, not in that very old one of ours. We have added them as an appendix because they have already been ascribed to this author previously. We leave it to the judgment of the Reader whether in fact the writers of the exemplar made the ascription unjustly.

Chapt. 46. *The Lord of the Hour.*

Hermes said, the lord of the hour in all nativities has all the significations common to the lord of the ASC. Wherefore, diligently seek out the lord of the hour of birth. For if it is direct, safe from impediments and from the inauspicious influx of the evil [planets], in an angle or the succedent of an angle, connected with the lucky stars either by ray or by body, especially if its nature is benefic, it denotes that the native will have a long, rich life, with many favors of fortune and nature, and increased by gifts, and the other good things that the lord of the ASC is accustomed to bestow when it is made fortunate. For, as Hermes testifies, the judgment is the same from either one of them.

Chapt. 47. *The Significations of the Planets in the Individual Houses of the Natal Chart.*

Planets in the Ascendant.

Saturn in the 1st house denotes difficulty in all [the native's] work and, death from ruin of the land[132] or from debt.

Jupiter [in the 1st signifies] honor, reverence, modesty, prudence, and a good life.

Mars [signifies] anger, war, and disputes.

The Sun, dominion, elevation, power, greatness of works and possessions, quick and solid learning.

Venus, joy, pleasure in eating and drinking, in ornaments, and clothes, love for women, gentle behaviour, beauty of body.

Mercury, wisdom, knowledge of writing and numbers.

The Moon, dominion, trips, removals to other locations, inconstancy, kindness towards the mother and great and noble ladies.

Planets in the Second House.

Saturn in the 2nd sign signifies the deterioration of [the native's] private property and of [his] livelihood and the loss of wealth through the interference of friends.

Jupiter [indicates] abundance of wealth and good intellectual capacity.

Mars, want, calamity, disturbances [caused] by slaves, and wounds.

The Sun, riches throughout his whole life, splendid status, and beautiful eyes.

Venus, abundant means and wealth from women.

Mercury, increase in riches and honor among kings.

The Moon, loss and damage of [the native's] private property and frequent changes of status.

---

132. The phrase *ruina terrae* 'ruin of the land' may refer to some financial disaster affecting the native's real estate, as his farm's being ruined by a flood, or, if taken literally, it could be translated 'falling in of earth', as sometimes happens to ditch-diggers when they are killed by the earthen walls of their ditch falling in upon them.

Planets in the Third House have These Significations.

Saturn, hatred between brothers and sisters.

Jupiter, happiness of brothers and sister and of relatives,   along with joy.

Mars,[133] hatred and contention of the brothers and sisters.

The Sun, some official duty from the king, trips.

Venus,   inconstancy and   bad luck   from bad   activities,   but many friends,   and   joy   from   them;   the   brothers   and   sisters   will be charming.

Mercury,   inclination and   readiness   to   learn   all   things;   the friends, brothers, and sisters will be strong.

The Moon,   official   duties and   joys from   rich men,   from kings, journeys, nobles, and foreigners.

Planets in the Fourth [House] Denote These Things.

Saturn,   disipation and loss   of   the   inheritance,   death   of the parents.

Jupiter,   utility from land,   inheritances,   buried treasures, and security from terrors.

Mars, outpouring of blood, homicide, a sad end.

The Sun, buried treasures,   revelation of secret and hidden things and arts, praise, dignity.

Venus,   a praiseworthy son, but one who in the beginning will have sadness because of his mother.

Mercury, a good memory, and skill in crafts.

The Moon, sorrow, but with a good end.

Planets in the Fifth [House] Portend These Things.

Saturn, dispersion and death of the children.

Jupiter, many good and upright children, advantage and praise from them, and riches from things hoped for.

Mars, many illegitimate children, and little joy from them.

The Sun, children of rank, and praise and fame in governing.

---

133. The printed text has 'Mercury' here in error (corrected in the Errata).

Venus, want and sorrow from one son at first, then joy from the children.

Mercury, much business from letters, good luck from one son.

The Moon, many children.

Planets in the Sixth [House] Signify These Things.

Saturn, illnesses, and a disobedient family.

Jupiter, few illnesses, advantage from cattle, and good luck from the family.

Mars, many hot and dry illnesses, a bad family.

The Sun, illnesses, disturbance [caused] by the slaves and low-born persons.

Venus, a covetous wife, illnesses from women, plundering by male and female slaves.

Mercury, deception and plundering by women on account of passion and intemperance.

The Moon, profit from animals.

Planets in the Seventh [House] Promise These Things.

Saturn, sadness in marriage, separation from the wife, a bad end.

Jupiter, joy from wives, and victory over enemies.

Mars, want, calamity, hard work, war, loss, sorrow, and disturbance in all things, and an inclination to passions.

The Sun, opposition from nobles, the rich, and the powerful.

Venus, joy from women, and success in things hoped for.

Mercury, craving and great temptations because of women, and quarrels with them.

The Moon, good things from women.

Planets in the Eighth [House] Denote These Things.

Saturn, inheritances from the death of relatives, and lengthy mourning.

Jupiter, loss of assets, but a good and praiseworthy end.

Mars, generally a bad death, or wounds in the hands and feet, disgrace, contempt, loss of assets, and great want.

The Sun, plundering of goods by powerful persons, a powerful and bad destruction [of assets] from business with kings

Venus, opposition to the mother, a long life, and a good death.

Mercury, enmities with neighbors, and mourning because of deaths, but increase in property, and great skill in crafts.

The Moon, the native, deposed from his official position and honor by kings or princes, will become a fugitive, and will experience many illnesses, want, and sadness.

Planets in the Ninth House of Heaven Indicate These Things.

Saturn, oppressive and terrible dreams, error in faith, illnesses, hindrances and losses in long journeys.

Jupiter, joy and good fortune in long journeys, good faith, true dreams, and [truthful] interpretation of them.

Mars, love of horses, wars, and wine, infidelity [in religion], and many worthless dreams, useless and harmful journeys.

The Sun, good personal philosophy, good faith, fear of God, and useful travel.

Venus, pleasure and good fortune through travel, religion, fear of God, true dreams, and [truthful] interpretation of them.

Mercury, learning, modesty, knowledge, and experience with many hidden things.

The Moon brings desire for travel to distant places, many bad thoughts.

Planets in the Midheaven Indicate These Things.

Saturn in a nocturnal geniture, great and manifest damages from kings and powerful men or a long captivity. But in a diurnal [nativity], riches and the exercise of great crafts, and a more fortunate status in old age than in youth.

Jupiter, riches, praise, and dignity.

Mars, sadness, and captivity by powerful men, poverty, wars, adversities.

The Sun, great fame, authority, usefullness among kings.

Venus, joy from kings and princes and noble women, offices, dignities, and the latter part of life moderately better than the earlier.

Mercury, great knowledge of writing, using numbers, and other arts, and excellent crafts.

The Moon, a great love for beautiful things, riches, offices, honors among kings and princes.

Planets in the Eleventh Sign Portend These Things.

Saturn, anxiety and pain from friends, hindrance of things wished for.

Jupiter, riches, praise, dignity through the agency of friends, overcoming enemies, advantage from things hoped for, good fidelity and faith. In a nocturnal birth, good fortune, fortitude, praise.

[Mars, little advancement, enmity of friends, loss of wealth, removal of faith.][134]

The Sun, joy and assistance from rich friends and from slaves, good fortune for the parents, an honest and famous name in outlying regions, good fortune in undertakings, favor and benevolence from men, and the latter time of life will be more fortunate in honors than the earlier.

Venus, good fortune from friends and close companions, good fidelity and faith, much wealth in the end of life.

Mercury, many friends [and] close companions, joy among wise men, generosity.

The Moon, joy from friends, and the fulfilment of every hope and expectation.

Planets in the Twelfth [House] Signify These Things.

Saturn, anxiety, captivity, hindrances from kings, terror in all things.

Jupiter, slavery, poverty, defection and sorrow from slaves.

Mars, illnesses, and damages from enemies, slaves, and base men, hindrances and misfortune in everything undertaken.

The Sun, enmities of kings, loss of honors, illnesses, want, and calamity from slaves, enemies, and low-born persons.

Venus, annoyances from bad women, and a bad marriage

Mercury, the native is wise, a philosopher, and very ingenious. But if it is impeded, [he is] frenzied, crazy, inquiring into

---

134. The printed text does not give any signification for Mars in this house. I have supplied the omission from Leopold, who summarizes Abu ‘Ali.

useless things, or perhaps a horse-trader, and a person knowing something about quadrupeds, and such like.

The Moon, hindrances from enemies, and, if she is made unfortunate by Saturn, captivity and poverty, a stinking mouth and body. But in a nocturnal birth, these evils will be mitigated.

Chapt. 48. *The Head and Tail of the Dragon of the Moon in the Twelve Houses of Heaven.*

The Head in the 1st house denotes domination and good fortune like its mixture with the planets. The Tail [denotes] trouble, decrease, and hindrance in all undertakings, and injury to one of the eyes.

The Head in the 2nd house, increase in property, and great good fortune. The Tail of the Dragon, poverty, and a fall from high [estate].

The Head in the 3rd house promises noble and fortunate brothers and true dreams. But the Tail, scattering of the brothers and sisters.

The Head in the 4th bestows usefulness and increase of farm lands, and inheritances. The Tail of the Dragon, diminution of the inheritance, and much hard work without any reward.

The Head in the 5th house, promises an increase in [the number of] children, and safety from all calamities. The Tail of the Dragon, loss and death of the children, and horrible accidents [befalling] them.

The Head in the 6th house, robustness against illnesses, many slaves, many animals, and profit from them. The Tail of the Dragon, illnesses, evildoing by the male and female slaves, and weakness among the animals, and no increase from them.

The Head in the 7th gives friendship with women. The Tail of the Dragon, dissolution of marriage, and powerful enemies.

The Head in the 8th, a sound and healthy life, and little fear. The Tail of the Dragon, a disgraceful death, and loss of good things.

The Head in the 9th indicates that the native's faith will be in accordance with the condition of the planets that are with it. The Tail of the Dragon, great changes, and bad faith.

The Head in the 10th house bestows good fortune on the native and an increase in his professional skill. The Tail of the Dragon, oppression, damages, unnecessary journeys.

The Head and the Tail of the Dragon in the 11th house give much hard work and little rest.

The Head in the 12th, strength and many enemies, an increase in evil things, and poverty. The Tail of the Dragon, little bad luck

against enemies, oppression of them, and [their] poverty, and no harm
from them.

Chapt. 49. *The Effects and Indications of the Part of Fortune in the Twelve Houses of the Natal Horoscope.*

When the Part of Fortune is in the 1st house, it signifies the
greatest good fortune in acuqiring wealth, and a prosperous outcome
in all business deals and contracts, games, and all other things for
which resources are commonly or can be provided.

In the 2nd it signifies the same things as in the 1st, but not so
perfectly.

In the 3rd, it gives good fortune in activities with brothers,
sisters, and kinsmen. And religious men will have a good monastery,
and entrance into a good order, and they will undertake short trips.

If it is in the 4th, it is favorable for the native to act in
common with his parents, to buy farms and houses, to work in mines,
to seek buried treasure and hidden things, to investigate arcane
things, to make wills and legacies.

If it is in the 5th house, it is good for the native to act in
common with his children, to tear off and put on clothes, to write
letters, to send couriers, to stage banquets and get-togethers, to
seek out pleasure and love affairs, to conduct business involving the
goods of children, or those things which pertain to children or
grandchildren.

In the 6th house, it is good to lease male and female slaves, for
they are made fortunate [by this position]. Also, to buy sheep, pigs,
and goats, to trade them, and to send them out to pasture, for they
are made fortunate. But one should not get angry with male or female
slaves or workmen, much less beat them, for they will win out.

In the 7th house, it is good to act in common with women, and to
seek love from them, to offer the property of women in order to make
a profit, and to do business with them. In particular, it is good to
change status, or to hand oneself over from one servitude to another,
or to remove from one place to another, in which you want to stay for
a while. For in that servitude or place it will go well with him, and
he will have good fortune. But wars ought to be avoided by whatever
means.

In the 8th house the Part of Fortune is badly placed, for [there]
it signifies loss. And this is the common opinion -- that the
opposition of the Part of Fortune signifies the greatest [degree] of
bad luck. When, therefore, the Part of Fortune is in the 8th house,
then its opposition is in the 2nd, which is the house of abundance.
Wherefore, at that time, you should not buy anything, nor sell
anything, nor play [games of chance], nor lend [to anyone], nor
should you serve as a guarantor. For all of these [actions] bring
damage and loss. But it is good to do business with things belonging
to your wife.

If it is in the 9th house, it is auspicious to undertake long journeys, to do business in foreign places, to deal with bishops and other religious magistrates, or to enroll in a religious order, or to seek benefactions or alms. Dreams that one has at this time are made fortunate, and you will perceive in yourself extraordinary inclinations of your mind towards God and many penetrating thoughts.

In the 10th, it is most fortunate to deal with kings, princes, and magistrates, especially to spend the money of princes for the sake of profit, or to do business with them, for it brings marvelous advantages. This time is the most suitable for commencing any art or craft, nor can any more fortunate time be found for seeking offices, honors, dignities, and for making laws. Then, it is a most fortunate [time] to obligate oneself to princes or to powerful men.

In the 11th house, judge in a manner similar to that which was mentioned in connection with the 10th. For although this house is weaker, nevertheless its own nature signifies the greatest good fortune in all things, with no exception. But especially it is auspicious then to seek money from princes, or to slay them. For the 11th house signifies the property of kings, princes, and lords.

If this Part is found in the 12th, it is good to buy horses, mules, asses, oxen, and cows, and to transact business concerning them, to send them to pasture, and to lend to others. It is also a fortunate [time] to give captives their freedom. But all other business activities undertaken for the sake of profit should be avoided, for they bring loss. Nor should one fight with enemies then, for at this time they gain strength, and their troops are encouraged, and they will obtain victory by the vote of Fortune.

Chapt. 50. *The Rest of the Accidental [Dignities or Debilities] of the Part of Fortune.*

When the Part of Fortune is in the exaltation of Saturn, the native will be fortunate among old men and slaves.

In the exaltation of Jupiter, among powerful men, nobles, and religious men.

In the exaltation of Mars, among princes, counts,[135] golden knights, and soldiers.

In the exaltation of the Sun, among kings and great princes.

[Its indication in the exaltation of Venus is missing.]

In the exaltation of Mercury, among teachers, secretaries, and public notaries.

---

135. I use this word to translate the Latin *comites* literally, 'companions' of the ruler or one of his deputies, but actually used in the Roman Empire to designate a variety of important administrative posts in the government. It eventually became a title of nobility in Europe.

In the exaltation of the Moon, among bath superintendents of lords, and virgins of humble stock.

Similarly, if the Part of Fortune is in the domicile or term of any planet, the native's fortune will lie among the same kind of men [as signified by that planet], but they will not be in so good a state as those above. And when the Part of Fortune is in an angle, it signifies great good fortune. In succedent [houses], good fortune through hard work. In cadent [houses], no luck at all, or very little. When the Sun makes a good aspect to the Part of Fortune, it increases the good fortune.

See also whether the Moon is with that same Part, and makes a conjunction or any aspect with its lord, and in whose domicile the Moon is. If it is in a domicile of Saturn, the native will have a cold nature, rarely bold and cheerful, and he will endure great labors. But if Saturn is oriental, a great inheritance will fall to him, and he will build new houses. But if the Moon is in a domicile of Jupiter, the native will be wise, prudent, and fortunate among powerful lords, and he will be loved by men. If this same [planet] is in a domicile of Mars, the native will be bold, will take delight in litigation, and will have his fortune among leaders of armies, counts, golden knights, and soldiers. If in the domicile of the Sun, the native will have many benefices from kings. If in a domicile of Venus, the native will be cheerful and skilled in music. In a domicile of Mercury, wise, skilled, prudent, crafty, and sly. You will judge in the same manner when the Moon is in the exaltations, or terms,.or aspects of these planets.

A Caution that must be Observed in Judgments.

In every signification, the following must be noted with extreme care: If it has a single testimony, it is commonplace. If two, it is stronger. If three, it is perfected, but only if the lords or significators are strong and not impedited.[136] Also, significations in cadent houses and mobile signs are weak. In succedent houses and common signs, stronger. In angles and fixed signs, strongest.

But if in any matter both good and evil signification and testimony fall together, compare one testimony with the other, whether it is stronger or weaker. For that which is stronger and has more dignities must be preferred. Observe it, therefore, and omit the other. But if it is equal on both sides, discard both of them.[137] For thus you will judge more surely and much more fortunately.

GLORY TO GOD ALONE!

---

136. This is an important and concise statement of a cardinal principle of astrological interpretation. It could be termed *reinforcement*.

137. This and the preceding sentence contain bad advice. Experience shows that astrological influences act independently. Each influence produces its own characteristic effect. If one is stronger, it will produce a greater effect, as compared to a weaker contrary influence, but the weaker influence will still operate. If they are equal in strength, then usually one gives a thing and the other takes it away. Examples abound. Superior earnings, offset by heavy expenses. A happy marriage, but a brief one. (Or two marriages -- one happy, and the other unhappy.) Achievement of high position, followed by its loss. Many illnesses, but good and effective medical treatment.

APPENDIX 1.

The Twelve Example Horoscopes.

Pingree notes that the example horoscopes given by Abu 'Ali are the same as those that his teacher Masha'allah included in his *Book of Nativities*.[138] We may therefore inquire where Masha'allah got them. The first step is to date the charts. Pingree has determined the dates of most of them. Three are from the *Pentateuch* of Dorotheus of Sidon (1st century). One is a 5th century chart from Rhetorius (early 6th century). The remaining eight are mostly 5th century charts, and Pingree conjectures that they may have been assembled by some Greek writer of the 6th century or later.

Some interesting questions arise. Why did Masha'allah use old Greek sources for his example charts rather than contemporary charts from the Arab world? Why did he take only three from the *Pentateuch*, which contains eight? Where did he get the one that is from Rhetorius? (Pingree says Rhetorius was not available in Arabic.) And where did he find the other eight?

Masha'allah was one of the first astrologers who wrote in Arabic. Not many had practiced the art in the Caliphate before him. It seems likely that he had no *Notable Nativities* of the 8th century from which to take examples. And I think he would not have dared to use the charts of prominent Muslims either living or of recent memory. Thus, it is possible that he used the old Greek charts out of necessity.

But it is also possible that the actual origin of the *Book of Nativities* is in the 6th century. Notice how the text begins.[139] "Masha'allah said that among all the books of astrology there is none to be found more useful than the *Book of Nativities* nor one so good in judgments." This may be merely an author's introduction to his own work, but it may also be a reference to an older work that the author is about to summarize or paraphrase for the reader. Perhaps among the Greek astrology books that the Arabs acquired was one written in the 6th century that summarized portions of the *Pentateuch* and added nativities collected by the author of the summary.

If that author was a working astrologer, or if he had access to the collections of contemporary astrologers, he may have had a group of fairly recent nativities to choose from. And he may have preferred to use more of them rather than to take a larger number of 400-year old ones from Dorotheus. It seems to me more likely that the whole collection of twelve charts was put together by a 6th century Greek than by an 8th or 9th century Arab.

---

138. *The Astrological History of Masha'allah*, Appendix 3.
139. *Op. cit.*, p. 145.

I also believe that Abu 'Ali's twelve charts were taken from the
same source used by Masha'allah and are not simply copies of the
charts in Masha'allah's *Book of Nativities*. Consequently, they
provide an independent witness to that source. Several of them are
corrupt and may, therefore, be misdated. I have marked their dates
with question marks in the translation and discussed some of the
problems below. In a few cases I have proposed alternative dates.

One final point. The rules contained in Abu 'Ali's book antedate
the charts. And, since the charts are only used to illustrate the
rules given in the text, it makes little difference whether they can
be dated or not. Any astrologer who intended to use the rules would
certainly try them out on his own collection of horoscopes.

Zodiacal Longitudes.

In checking the planetary positions given in the charts, it is
preferable to use positions that are similar to those used by the
astrologers who drew the original charts. We may reasonably assume
that the charts from the *Pentateuch* were based on the Hellenistic
zodiac, which was about 5° in advance of the tropical zodiac in the
early 1st century. The later charts, however, would have been
calculated with Ptolemy's *Handy Tables*. These tables were wrong to
start with, since Ptolemy had the equinox in the wrong place.[140] The
difference between Ptolemaic and tropical longitudes was a little
over a degree in Ptolemy's own time and steadily increased
thereafter. By the middle of the 5th century it was approaching 3°. I
have used my own computer programs to calculate tropical longitudes
(plus 5°) for the earlier charts and Ptolemaic longitudes for the
later ones. The "Ptolemaic" longitudes are not quite identical to
those that can be obtained from the *Handy Tables*, since they are
calculated directly from the theory and consequently have a higher
formal precision than the *Handy Tables*.

Pingree has used tropical longitudes for his comparisons, which is
wrong in every case. The difference is noticeable when planets are at
the beginning or end of a sign. For example, in Chart No. 3 Dorotheus
has Saturn in Virgo. Pingree has 28 Leo (it should be 26 Leo), but
the Hellenistic longitude is 1 Virgo. In that same chart Dorotheus
has Venus in Taurus. Pingree gives 27 Taurus (it should be 26
Taurus). The Hellenistic longitude is 1 Gemini. This lends some
weight to dating the chart 1 April 36 instead of 2 Apr 36. Again, in
Chart. 4 Dorotheus has Saturn in Pisces. Pingree has it in 29
Aquarius. The Hellenistic longitude is 3 or 4 Pisces.

---

140. A fact unknown to Neugebauer and Van Hoesen (*Greek Astrology*, p.172), who mistakenly
assumed the tables had zero error in the 2nd century.

Celestial Houses.

Masha'allah's Charts 1,2,8-12 have MC's and intermediate house cusps according to the so-called Alchabitius system,[141] but Abu 'Ali never mentions anything but the ASC. I have therefore drawn the charts according to the Sign-House system unless he mentions a precise degree for the ASC, in which case I have drawn the chart according to the Equal House system. This is admittedly arbitrary, for Abu 'Ali seems to vacillate between the two systems. A careful study of his text and his comments on the charts might shed some more light on the matter.

Notes on Individual Charts.

Chart 1.

This chart is from Dorotheus, *Pentateuch*, i. 24. Pingree dates it to 2 Aug 43, but 3 Aug 43 is equally possible. The LMT was approximately 1 AM.

Chart 2.

The source of this chart is unknown. Pingree dates it to 29 Jan 425, but 30 Jan 425 is also possible. The LMT was approximately 10:30 AM. If the date is correct, then both Mercury and Venus are misplaced, for Mercury was actually in Capricorn and Venus in Sagittarius.

Chart 3.

This chart is from Dorotheus, *Pentateuch* i. 24. Pingree dates it to 2 Apr 36, but 1 Apr 36 would put Venus more securely in Taurus. The LMT was approximately 9 PM. It is Abu 'Ali's 3rd chart, but Masha'allah's 4th. If the date is correct, then Mercury and Mars are misplaced, for Mercury was actually in Taurus and Mars in Pisces, but the same errors appear in the Arabic version of Dorotheus.

Chart 4.

This chart is from Dorotheus, *Pentateuch* i. 24. Pingree dates it to 30 Mar 22, but 29 Mar 22 is equally possible. The LMT was approximately 11 AM. It is Abu 'Ali's 4th chart, but Masha'allah's 3rd. If the date is correct, then Venus and Mars are misplaced, for Venus in Virgo is impossible (it was actually in Aquarius), and Mars was in Cancer. The Arabic version of Dorotheus has the same error for Venus and does not give the position of Mars.

---

141. Which, since it first appears in a work by Rhetorius, should perhaps be renamed the Rhetorius system, although he may well have adopted it from some still earlier writer.

Chart 5.

This chart is from an unknown source. Pingree dates it doubtfully to 9 Nov 542. The LMT was approximately 9 PM. (Masha'allah's chart has Jupiter and the Moon in Virgo rather than Gemini. Pingree dates it to 2 Nov 747.) It seems to me that a better solution is 6 Nov 423. On this date Venus was in Libra (instead of the impossible Leo of the text), Saturn was in Libra, and Mars was in the beginning of Aquarius instead of Leo, which is not so good a match as the positions given by Pingree, but this date fits in with the others in the early 400's.

	Masha'allah	Abu 'Ali	6 Nov 423	9 Nov 542
Sun	Sco	Sco	13 Sco 10	16 Sco 54
Moon	Vir	Gem	16 Gem 37	28 Tau 40
Mercury	Sco	Sco	7 Sco 33	21 Sco 39
Venus	Leo	Leo	19 Lib 43	27 Sag 14
Mars	Leo	Leo	1 Aqu 48	0 Leo 15
Jupiter	Vir	Gem	6 Gem 25	21 Gem 41
Saturn	Sco	Sco	28 Lib 52	12 Sco 08

The commentaries by Masha'allah and Abu 'Ali both state that Mercury and Saturn are cadent. Abu 'Ali adds that Jupiter is in the 11th house. None of this is true of the charts they give. And if Abu 'Ali is right about Jupiter, then both of the dates given above are impossible. Further research is needed.

Chart 6.

This chart is from an unknown source. Pingree dates it to 25 Mar 434, but 24 Mar 434 is equally possible. The LMT was approximately 10 PM. If the date is correct, then Mercury and Saturn are misplaced, for Mercury was in Pisces and Saturn in Aquarius.

	Masha'allah	Abu 'Ali	24 Mar 434	25 Mar 434
Sun	Ari	Psc	2 Ari 47	3 Ari 45
Moon	Psc	Psc	9 Psc 22	22 Psc 19
Mercury	Ari	Ari	7 Psc 08	7 Psc 57
Venus	Tau	Tau	15 Tau 52	16 Tau 56
Mars	Vir	Vir	7 Leo 31	7 Leo 33
Jupiter	Ari	Ari	12 Ari 29	12 Ari 43
Saturn	Psc	Psc	27 Aqu 51	27 Aqu 57

The commentaries say that the Sun, Jupiter, and Saturn are all angular. With a 45° spread between Saturn and Jupiter, they can't be. (Also, these triplicity rulers belong to the Fire triplicity, so Masha'allah's Sun in Aries is preferable to Abu 'Ali's Sun In Pisces.) Further research is needed.

Chart 7.

This chart is from an unknown source. Pingree dates it to 18 Oct
439, but his Moon position is for 19 Oct 439, which is the correct
date. The LMT was approximately 7 AM. It is Abu 'Ali's 7th chart, but
Masha'allah's 8th. There are large errors in the longitudes of
several of the planets.

	Masha'allah	Abu 'Ali	19 Oct 439
Sun	6 Lib 08	8 Lib	24 Lib 14
Moon	29 Leo	26 Leo	29 Leo 38
Mercury	11 Sco	11 Sco 15	11 Sco
Venus	28 Vir	-	27 Vir
Mars	18 Vir	18 Vir	17 Vir
Jupiter	21 Lib	21 Lib 12	3 Lib
Saturn	11 Tau	15 Tau	8 Tau
N. Node	8 Tau	8 Tau 40	28 Tau 41

Chart 8.

This chart is from an unknown source. Pingree dates it to 19 Jan
403, but 20 Jan is better because the Sun was in 0 Aqu 07 on that
date whereas it was in 29 Cap 06 on the 19th. The LMT was
approximately 9 PM. It is Abu 'Ali's 8th chart, but Masha'allah's
7th.

Chart 9.

This chart is from an unknown source. Pingree dates it to 25 Nov
464. The LMT was approximately 5 AM.

	Masha'allah	Abu 'Ali	25 Nov 464
Sun	8 Sag	9 Sag	2 Sag 54
Moon	16 Ari	16 Ari	9 Ari 46
Mercury	21 Sco	21 Sco	21 Sag 15
Venus	12 Sco	13 Sco	16 Sco 34 Rx
Mars	15 Sag	19 Sag	19 Sag 09
Jupiter	23 Sco	22 Sco	12 Sco 47
Saturn	14 Psc	15 Psc	3 Psc 37
N. Node	23 Cap	23 Cap	23 Cap 00

Chart 10.

This chart is from Rhetorius and appears as Chapt. 12 in Parisinus
graecus 2506 (ed. in CCAG VIII.1). Neugebauer and Van Hoesen (*Greek
Horoscopes*, pp. 138-140) date it to 8 Sep 428 at approximately 10 PM
LMT [9:15 PM is closer]. Rhetorius gives no interpretation, but uses
the chart to illustrate a method of house division. It would appear
to have been drawn for Constantinople. The planetary positions were
accurately calculated from Ptolemy's tables as can be seen from the
following comparison.

	Rhetorius	Ptolemy	Masha'allah	Abu 'Ali
Sun	14 Vir 19	14 Vir 20	17 Vir	17 Vir
Moon	3 Psc 04	3 Psc 06	3 Psc	1 Psc
Mercury	3 Lib 37	3 Lib 33	4 Lib	5 Lib
Venus	25 Leo 40	25 Leo 34	25 Leo	17 Leo
Mars	21 Vir 06	21 Vir 23	-- Vir	21 Vir
Jupiter	15 Lib 41	15 Lib 40	16 Lib	17 Lib
Saturn	14 Sag 21	14 Sag 29	14 Sag	14 Sag
N. Node	3 Cap 41	3 Cap 36	8 Cap	8 Cap
ASC	25 Tau 16		11 Tau	21 Tau

It is interesting to note that Abu 'Ali gives the degree and sign of Mars, while Masha'allah gives only the sign.

The chart from Rhetorius originally had house cusps calculated according to a variation of the Alchabitius system. The 6th house cusp was 14 Libra, so only Jupiter was in the 6th house. Masha'allah's chart has been changed to make the ASC degree 11 Taurus, in order to put Mercury in the 6th house to agree with the commentary.

Despite the fact that the text of both authors says the planets are in the 6th house from the Part of Fortune, they are not. Both authors have treated the chart as if the planets were in the 6th house from the ASC. But this is a bad position as we have just seen in the preceding horoscope. I believe some words have dropped out of the Arabic text used by both Masha'allah and Abu 'Ali, and I have made a conjectural restoration in the translation (q.v.).

Chart 11.

This chart is from an unknown source. Pingree dates it to 7 Feb 442. The LMT was approximately 9:30 PM. The positions of the Sun and the Part of Fortune are in error by several degrees.

	Masha'allah	Abu 'Ali	7 Feb 442
Sun	18 Aqu	10 Aqu	18 Aqu 35
Moon	18 Can	8 Can 04	5 Can 53
Mercury	17 Aqu	15 Aqu	16 Aqu 18
Venus	14 Psc	25 Psc	24 Psc 48
Mars	16 Sag	15 Sag	16 Sag 57
Jupiter	15 Sco	15 Sag	15 Sag 42
Saturn	10 Gem	2 Gem	2 Gem 22
N. Node	14 Ari	---	14 Ari 03
ASC	11 Lib	2 Lib 30	

Chart 12.

    This chart is from an unknown source. Pingree says Abu 'Ali's
positions are undatable and proposes a date of 16 Apr 455, which puts
Saturn in Scorpio, Jupiter in Capricorn (Pingree says 0 Aquarius),
and the Node in Cancer. I think this is wrong, for the commentary
plainly requires Saturn in Libra. I offer another date, which puts
Mars in the wrong sign, but is satisfactory otherwise. The reader can
choose between the two or find another that he prefers.

	Masha'allah	Abu 'Ali	3 Apr 394	17 Apr 455
Sun	24 Ari	24 Ari	11 Ari 48	25 Ari 11
Moon	16 Lib	17 Lib	17 Lib 56	13 Lib 52
Mercury	-	-	16 Psc 55	28 Ari 51
Venus	-	-	24 Tau 30	21 Ari 42
Mars	2 Sag	- Sag	24 Tau 54	20 Sag 37
Jupiter	2 Sag	17 Sag	2 Sag 12	28 Cap 46
Saturn	27 Lib	27 Lib	27 Lib 15	22 Sco 16
N. Node	1 Sco	17 Sco	9 Sco 48	28 Can 55

Final Comment.

    The reader may wonder why there are so many errors in these
charts. We cannot, of course, rule out the possibility that some
errors were made by the astrologers who first drew the charts, but
most of the errors are probably due to mistakes made by the long
chain of copyists and translators through whose hands they have
passed. Remember that they were originally in Greek, then translated
into Arabic, and from Arabic into Latin. They may also have been
copied several times in each language. Thus, between the Greek
astrologers who drew the original charts and and the editors of the
Latin versions (Heller and Pingree) there was a string of from 5 to
10 copyists and translators, anyone of whom could have made one or
more mistakes.

    Readers who like puzzles can study the inconsistencies in these
charts and possibly deduce more accurate dates for some of them.   If
so, some slight improvement might be possible in the commentaries
that accompany each chart. But the main gain would be historical not
astrological. I repeat what I said above. The charts are merely used
for illustration of the rules. Any chart will serve that purpose, so
long as accurate biographical data is available for the native.
Readers who dislike puzzles can ignore the charts with discrepancies
and substitute some from their own collections.

APPENDIX 2.

MASHA'ALLAH'S BOOK OF NATIVITIES.

[Chapt. 1.] *Whether the Child Will [Live to] be Weaned or Not.*

Masha'allah said that among all the books of astrology there is not one found more useful than the *Book of Nativities* nor one so good in judgments. He who is versed in it will find knowledge and wisdom in it, and he will delight in its practical knowledge.

First, it should be known whether the child will [live to] be weaned or not. And you will know this from the ASC, namely from the lords of its triplicity, and from the lords of the domicile of the Sun if the nativity is diurnal, or of the domicile of the Moon if it is nocturnal; and from the lord of the New Moon or the lord of the Full Moon if he was born after the New Moon or the Full Moon.

And if it is from the New Moon or the Full Moon, you will look at the lords of its triplicity. And in addition, you will look at Jupiter and Venus. And if the nativity is diurnal, you will look at the diurnal planets; and if it is nocturnal, at the nocturnal planets.

And you will begin to look at the [first] lord of the triplicity of the 1st house, i.e. the ASC, and at the second lord, and at the third lord; these are the lords of the triplicity of the first [house]. And if they are free [from any aspect of] the evil [planets], in the ASC namely, or in the 10th house or in the 11th or in the 5th, the native will live.

But if they are cadent from the angles and are infortunes, you will look at the lords of the triplicity of the Sun's domicile if it is a diurnal nativity. But if it is a nocturnal nativity, you will look at the lords of the triplicity of the Moon's domicile. And if they are in a good house and safe from [any aspect of] the evil [planets], the native will live.

But if they are in bad houses and are infortunes, you will look at the lords of the triplicity of the domicile of the Part of fortune. And if it is in a good house and free from [any aspect of] the evil [planets], the native will live.

But if it is a diurnal nativity, you will look at the Part of Fortune; and if it is nocturnal, you will look at the Moon. And if it is in an evil house, you will look at the lords of the triplicity of the domicile of the conjunction of the sun and the Moon if the nativity was around the New Moon. Or you will look at the lords of the triplicity of the domicile of the Full Moon if the nativity was around the Full Moon. And if they are angular and free from [any

aspect of] the evil [planets], the native will live. But if they are
evil [planets] and impedited, then look at Jupiter, which is a helper
in nativities. And if it is in an angle or in a succedent of an angle
and free from [any aspect of] the evil [planets], he will live. But
if it is in an evil house and impedited by an evil [planet], you will
look at Venus. And if it is in an angle or in a succedent of an angle
and free from [any aspect of] the evil [planets], he will live. But
if it is in an evil house and impedited by infortunes,[1] you will look
at the Moon. And if it is in the ASC or the 10th house and free from
[any aspect of] the evil [planets], [and] it is joined to a diurnal
star if the nativity is diurnal or joined to a nocturnal star if the
nativity is nocturnal, and it is free from [any aspect of] the evil
[planets], he will live. But if it is evilly [placed], you will look
at the Almuten.

   And you will know from the lords of the triplicity of the ASC; and
if it is a diurnal nativity, from the lords of the triplicity of the
Sun; and if it is a nocturnal nativity, from the lords of the
triplicity of the Moon; and from the lords of the triplicity of the
domicile of the conjunction of the Sun and the Moon, if the nativity
is around the New Moon; or by the lords of the triplicity of the
domicile of the Full Moon, if the nativity is before the New Moon.
And if they are in angles or in succedents of angles and free from
[any aspect of] the evil [planets], he will live. But if they are in
evil houses and impedited, he will die.

   Then, you will look at the planet that is Almuten, and the one to
which it communicates its disposition, and how many degrees are
between them. And if it is in a fixed sign, you will give one year to
eah degree; and if it is in a common sign, you will give a month to
each degree; and if it is in a mobile sign, you will give a day to
each degree. But if the Almuten is cadent, and an evil planets is in
the ASC, and the Moon is joined to an evil [planet], he will live as
much time as there are degrees. That is, if the receiver of the
disposition is impedited and in a fixed sign, they will be years; and
if in a common sign, months; and if in a mobile sign, days.

   Then, look at the degrees of the Sun or the Moon. If either of
them aspects the Almuten by square or conjoins it in the same
domicile or opposes it, it will be evil unless the degrees of *Athazer*
are there.[2] And, if any of the degrees of *Athazer* are there, he will
live as many years or months or days (as is said above) as there are
degrees.[3] And if the Almuten is joined to an evil [planet] by the
square or opposition aspect, and no fortune aspects it, the newborn

---

   1. Literally, 'by afflicted [planets]', but I think he means the evil planets.
   2. This word is from the Arabic *al-tasyirat* 'starting-points' used to translate the Greek
apheses. It designates a series of elongations of the Moon from the Sun that were considered
significant in certain cases. Wright gives the list: 0°, 12°, 45°, 90°, 135°, 168°, 180°, 192°,
225°, 270°, 315°, and 348° (Al-Biruni, *The Book of Instruction*, Sect. 254, n. 1). These numbers are
simply the usual Moon phases (conjunction, 1st quarter, etc.) along with half-phases or octants
(half way between New Moon and 1st quarter, etc.). To these are added the 12° points on either side
of the conjunction, which mark the approximate points where the Moon becomes visible or invisible.
And, for the sake of symmetry, 12° points on either side of the opposition.
   3. That is, if the number of degrees between the significators coincides with one of the *Athazer*
numbers, he will live that number of years, months, or days.

will live. But if the Moon is configured between two evil [planets]
and one of them is in the ASC, the other is in the 7th, and the Moon
badly [situated] in an angle, it will die.

But [if] the lords of the triplicity of the ASC or the lords of
the triplicity of the Sun's domicile, and the lords of the triplicity
of the Part of Fortune's domicile, and the lords of the triplicity of
the domicile of the New Moon or the Full Moon, are impedited or
cadent, and any planet is in [a position of] strength, he will have
serious illnesses. And if the lords of the triplicity of the
ascending sign are cadent, he will die. And it will be worse if one
of the aforesaid is Saturn in a nocturnal nativity or Mars in a
diurnal nativity, namely in one of the angles.

But if the Moon is received and the lord of the ASC is in a good
house, he will live, and he will be honored, and he will have many
brothers. But if there is no reception, it indicates poverty.

If the Part of Fortune is with the Moon, and aspects Venus in a
nocturnal nativity or Jupiter in a diurnal nativity, it indicates
high position and life, just as when the Part of Fortune is in a good
house.

Every planet that is a significator, and is oriental in a diurnal
nativity and in a masculine sign or is occidental in a nocturnal
nativity and in a feminine sign, will have good strength, and its
testimony will be good, and it indicates high status for the native.

But if the lord of the ASC or the Moon is in an evil [house] and
the lord of the domicile of the Moon is in an angle, it indicates
death.

And when you know that the native will not live long, you will
make *Athazer* from the ASC degree up to the evil planet that
impedites, and you will give to each sign one month. But if the
native makes it through these months, he will live as many years as
the months that were predicted.

Then, look at the lord of the 5th house. If it is in a good house,
the prediction must be judged good; if in an evil [house], it will
narrow his own soul in poverty.

When there is a Hyleg in the Nativity and when Not.

[Chapt. 2.] *The Hyleg in the Knowledge of Life: When the Nativityof
the Child Indicates Life.*

And when you want to know this, select[4] the Sun as Hyleg in a
diurnal nativity. And if it is in an angle or in a succedent of an
angle and in a masculine sign or in a masculine quarter -- i.e, from
the 1st house to the MC --[5] and the lord of the domicile aspects it,
or the lord of the term, or the lord of the exaltation or the lord of

---

4. Reading *elige* 'select' instead of *dirige* 'direct'.
5. The printed text has '7th house forwards', but the 7th house is in a feminine quarter.

the triplicity or of the face, it will be the Hyleg. And if none of
these aspects it, it will not be the Hyleg.

Then, you will look at the Moon. And if it is in an angle or in a
succedent of an angle, and in a feminine sign or in a feminine
quarter, and it is aspected just as I said in the case of the Sun,
you will accept it as the Hyleg.

But if the Sun or the Moon is not the Hyleg, you will look at the
lord of the domicile of the New Moon or the Full Moon. If it is not
the Hyleg, you will look at the lord of the domicile of the Part of
Fortune. And if you don't find this to be the Hyleg, you will put the
ASC degree for the Hyleg, if the lord of the ASC aspects the ASC. But
if all the aforesaid fail, there will be no Hyleg.

The Indication of Time from the Alcochoden.

[Chapt. 3.] *The Alcochoden, through Which is Known the Computation
[of the Length] of Life.*

And when the Hyleg has been found, you will look at the
Alcochoden. And you will look at the Hyleg and the lord of its terms,
and the lord of its triplicity, and the lord of its domicile, and the
lord of its exaltation, and the lord of its face. And the one of
these that aspects the Hyleg will be the Alcochoden. But if one or
two or three of the planets aspect the Hyleg, the planet that is most
dignified and nearer in degrees will be the Alcochoden.

You may know that when the Sun is in Aries or Leo, it will be the
Hyleg and the Alcochoden.⁶ Similarly, if the Moon is in Taurus or in
Cancer, it will be the Hyleg and the Alcochoden whether they aspect
it or not, and similarly with the Sun.

And when you have found the Alcochoden, look at it. If it is in an
angle⁷ or in its own domicile or in its exaltation of triplicity,
safe from any impediment, namely from retrogradation or from
combustion by the Sun, you will give it the major years of the
planet. And if it is in a succedent of an angle, and safe from [any
aspect of] the evil [planets], you will give it the middle years. But
if it is in a cadent from an angle, and has no dignity there, you
will give it the minor years.

And you may know that an augment of the years of a planet or a
diminution of them does not take place except through the strength of
the planet or through its debility. But if the planet is oriental and
in good state, you will give the greater years. And if it is not
oriental, and it has an evil aspect with one [of the planets], you
will give it the minor years. And if it is occidental, and has an
evil aspect with one [of the planets], and is retrograde, you will
give it as many weeks as minor years. And if it is in an evil house
in which it cannot be worse when retrograde [and is aspected by one]

---

6. The MS has *erit alcoden erit yles alcoden*, for which read *erit yles et alcoden*.
7. The MS has *ex gradibus* 'of degrees' after 'angle' by mistake.

of the lighter planets, you will   give it   as many days as are the
minor years of the planet.

And you may know that when the Head of the Dragon is in the same
sign with the planet which is Almuten, less than 12 degrees either
before or after, it adds a fourth part of the years of the planet
that is Almuten; and if it is closer in degrees, it will be more
effective. But if the Tail of the Dragon is there, it takes away a
fourth part of the years. And if it is in partile [conjunction] with
the Sun or the Moon, it takes away nothing. But if the Sun is the
Alcochoden and is some distance away from it, it takes awy from its
years. Ptolemy said, The Head with the fortunes adds good fortune,
and the Tail takes away from the years.• But if the Head or the Tail
is with the Sun or the Moon, the strength [of the nodes] will appear
either for good or evil, and more strongly in the case of the Moon.

But if Jupiter is in the ASC with Venus, each one of these adds
its own minor years in the nativity unless the infortunes impedite
them and the Moon is similarly in a bad state. But if one of the
aforesaid fortunes, viz. Jupiter and Venus, is the lord of the house
of death, and is in the ASC, the newborn will die before it lives.

How Many Years the Planets Add to the Alcochoden.

[Chapt. 4.] [How] to Know What the Planets Add or Subtract.

And when you know how many years you ought to put for the
Alcochoden, and you want to know how many are taken away or added,
look at the Alcochoden. If there is a fortune with it and it aspects
it by sextile or any other good aspect, and if it is in a good house,
it will increase the minor years of that fortune. But if the fortunes
that aspect the Alcochoden are weak, in place of the minor years you
will give the same [number of] months. And if the fortunate planet
that aspects the Alcochoden is retrograde, and an evil [planet]
impedites it, there will be days in the same number as the minor
years.

But if an infortune is with the Alcochoden, and that star will be
the receiver of the degrees of the Alcochoden, and they aspect each
other by square aspect or by opposition, and they have a conjunction
with the lord of the house of death, there will be hours in the same
number as the minor years of the Alcochoden. But if Mercury is in a
good house and aspects the Alcochoden with a good aspect, its minor
years will be an increment for it. And if it is the converse, it will
be reduced by the number of [Mercury's] minor years. And the
strongest of the planetary aspects with the Alcochoden is the aspect
of Mars. But if you want to know the [time of] death with certainty,
look at the evil [planet] that impedites the Alcochoden; and when the
Alcochoden comes to those degrees [by direction], he will die.

---

8. Not in the *Tetrabiblos* or in pseudo-Ptolemy's *Centiloquy*. Perhaps in one of the spurious
works attributed to Ptolemy.

Translator's Comment.

I think those who take the trouble to read these chapters of Masha'allah's work and compare them with the corresponding chapters of Abu 'Ali will be able to judge whether the latter author "simply reiterates his master's message" as Pingree puts it. Abu 'Ali covers the same ground as Masha'allah, but in my opinion his work is considerably superior on several counts. No doubt the master would have been proud of his pupil.

GLOSSARY

Accidental Debility. A position in the circle of houses, a
    characteristic of motion, or a configuration which decreases
    the strength of a planet. For example, being cadent or in the
    8th house, being retrograde, or being in bad aspect with a
    malefic.

Accidental Dignity. A position in the circle of houses, a
    characteristic of motion, or a configuration which increases
    the strength of a planet. For example, being in the ASC or MC,
    being swift in motion, or being in good aspect to a benefic.

Afflicted. Said of a planet, cusp, or Part when it is badly aspected
    by one or more malefic (q.v.) planets.

Alchabitius Houses. An ancient system of house division that is named
    for the author of a popular medieval treatise on astrology.

Alcochoden. A Persian term designating a dispositor of the Hyleg
    (q.v.) chosen according to a special rule explained in Chapt.
    3.

Alictisal. An Arabic term signifying a planet that is applying to
    conjunction with another planet.

Almuten. An Arabic term signifying the strongest planet having
    rulership over a particular house.

Angle. One of the principal houses of the horoscope, viz. the ASC,
    MC, DSC, and IMC (1st, 10th, 7th, and 4th).

Angle of the Earth. The IMC or 4th house.

Application. An aspect between two planets that is within orbs (q.v.)
    and approaching exactitude.

ASC. The Ascendant or 1st house of a chart.

ASC Degree. The ascending degree or cusp of the 1st house.

Aspect. A visual angle between two points in the zodiac, viz. a
    conjunction, sextile, square, trine, or opposition. (The
    conjunction is not an aspect, strictly speaking, but is
    included with the aspects for convenience.)

Athazer. An Arabic term for a series of elongations of the Moon from
    the Sun that were considered significant in certain cases. See
    the footnote to the word in Masha'allah's Book of Nativities,
    Chapt. 1.

Bad House. *See* Evil House.

Benefic. One of the "good" planets, Jupiter and Venus.

Besieged. Said of a point in the zodiac when it is between two
        planets. This can be corporally or by aspect.

Cadent House. The 3rd, 6th, 9th, and 12th houses are cadent.

Cadent Planet. A planet posited in a cadent house.

Caput. *See* Dragon's Head.

Cauda. *See* Dragon's Tail.

Chart. An astrological diagram of the celestial houses and the
        planets they contain. In Western astrology it represents the
        sky as it would appear to an observer facing south. The houses
        begin at the eastern horizon and are numbered downward in a
        counter-clockwise direction. The form of the chart has varied.
        The oldest charts known are round, but the square form was
        standard during the middle ages and the early modern period.
        The round chart, which is easier to read, is the modern
        standard.

Circle (of Houses). A reference to the celestial houses, of which the
        ASC is the first.

Combust. Said of a planet when it is within 8°30' of the Sun.

Common Sign. One of the four signs, Gemini, Virgo, Sagittarius, or
        Pisces.

Configured (with). Aspected (by).

Conjunction. A configuration in which two points are either in the
        same degree of the zodiac or within a few degrees of each
        other. The points can be planets, house cusps, parts, fixed
        stars, etc. The word is also used to refer to the conjunction
        of the Sun and Moon (i.e., the New Moon), especially in the
        phrase "the preceding conjunction," which refers to the new
        Moon that preceded the moment for which a chart is drawn. (*See*
        New Moon Nativity.)

Cusp. The point in the zodiac where a house begins.

Debilitated. Said of a planet in a debility (q.v.).

Debility. A position or configuration that decreases the strength of
        a planet.
        There are two kinds: accidental and essential (qq.v.).

Derived House. A house in a circle of houses that begins with a house
        other than the ASC or 1st house. For example, the 9th house is
        the House of Marriage of Brothers because it is the 7th house
        (marriage) from the 3rd (brothers).

Detriment. The sign opposite the sign ruled by a planet. A planet in
    its detriment is weak.

Dignified. Said of a planet when it is well-placed in the zodiac or
    the circle of houses or through some other circumstance.

Dignity. A position or configuration that increases the strength of a
    planet. There are two kinds: accidental and essential (qq.v.).

Direct. Said of a planet when it is moving forward in the zodiac.

Direction. See Progression.

Diurnal Nativity. A natal horoscope with the Sun above the horizon.

Diurnal Planet. One of the planets that is said to "rejoice" by day,
    viz. the Sun, Jupiter, and Saturn. Mercury is diurnal when it
    rises before the Sun.

Domicile. A sign of the zodiac. (Used in this translation to render
    the Latin word domus 'house' when it refers to a sign rather
    than to a celestial house.)

Dragon's Head (of the Moon). The Moon's ascending node.

Dragon's Tail (of the Moon). The Moon's descending node.

Dry Signs. The fire and earth signs: Aries, Taurus, Leo, Virgo,
    Sagittarius, and Capricorn.

DSC. The Descendant or 7th house of a chart.

Ductoria. A Persian term signifying a position of power for a planet.
    See Chapt. 16 and note 67. Variant spelling of dustoria (q.v.).

Dustoria. A Persian term signifying a position of power for a planet.
    See Chapt. 6 and note 24. Less accurately spelled ductoria
    (q.v.).

Election. An astrological chart erected for the moment when someone
    proposes to begin some undertaking. Within the available time-
    span, a moment is chosen which puts all the signs, planets, and
    parts in the best possible positions.
    This branch of astrology is related to both Horary and Natal
    astrology.

Elevated. Said of a planet when it is in the upper part of the chart.

Elevated above. Said of a planet when it is higher in the chart than
    another planet.

Equal House. A modern name for the second oldest system of house
    division. It puts the cusps of the houses at multiples of 30°
    from the ASC degree.

Essential Debility. A position in the zodiac where a planet loses
    strength by virtue of non-rulership or opposition to a major

rulership. There are three such positions: detriment, fall, and
peregrine (qq.v.).

Essential Dignity. A position in the zodiac where a planet gains
strength by virtue of its rulership. There are five such
positions: sign, exaltation, term, triplicity, and face
(qq.v.).

Evil. Bad, as the opposite of good. This word is preferred to "bad"
because it can be either an adjective or a noun.

Evil House. The 6th, 8th, and 12th houses are evil because they rule
sickness, death, and secret enemies.

Exaltation. A sign in which a planet has special strength.

Face. One of the 36 10-degree subdivisions of the zodiac. Usually
called "decan" by modern astrologers. There are three to a
sign, and their rulers are assigned in the classical order of
the planets, beginning with Mars for the first face of Aries,
the Sun for the second face, etc.

Fall. The sign opposite the sign of Exaltation (q.v.) of a planet. A
planet in its fall is weak.

Feminine Quarter. (Chapt. 2) The quadrant from the MC to the DSC and
the one opposite it are feminine.

Feminine Sign. One of the even-numbered signs: Taurus, Cancer, etc.

Figure. An obsolescent term for chart (q.v.).

First Lord of the Triplicity. See Triplicity.

Five Dignities. See Dignity.

Fixed Sign. One of the four signs, Taurus, Leo, Scorpio, or Aquarius.

Fixed Star. A star as distinguished from a planet. The stars visible
to the naked eye are so far away that their movements are
imperceptible to the casual observer; hence, they appear to be
"fixed" in their constellations.

Fortune. One of the fortunate planets, Jupiter and Venus.

Friendly Rays. Good aspects (q.v.).

Full Moon Nativity. A natal horoscope for which the preceding
lunation was a full Moon.

Good House. The angular houses and the 3rd, 5th, 9th, and 11th houses
are good.

Head. See Dragon's Head.

Horary Chart. An astrological chart erected for the moment when a
question is asked. It is used to obtain information pertaining

to the person asking the question, his circumstances, and the answer to his question. A horary chart can also be drawn for the moment when something happened and used to judge the attendant circumstances and the outcome. Such a chart is properly called "a chart set for a time certain," but in ordinary usage it is usually called simply "a horary chart."

Horoscope. An astrological chart. Originally, it meant the Egyptian asterism rising on the eastern horizon at a specific moment. In the classical period it meant the ASC. In modern usage, it ordinarily refers to a birth chart.

House. One of the 12 divisions of the horoscope chart. In the older astrologers, it can also mean "sign (of a planet)." But in the present translation "domicile" is used in that sense. Ordinarily, houses are reckoned from the ASC, but they can also be reckoned from any other house, the Part of Fortune, or one of the lights.

Hyleg. A Persian term for the prorogator that governs the life of the Native. *See* Chapt. 2, note 12.

IMC. The *Imum Caeli* or 4th house of a chart.

Impedited. Literally, "hindered." It refers to a planet that is weak or unfortunate because of its zodiacal position or house position or because it receives an unfavorable aspect, especially from a Malefic (q.v.).

Influence. The astrological force of a planet.

Infortune. A malefic planet.

Lights. The Sun and the Moon.

Light of Time. The Sun in a diurnal chart and the Moon in a nocturnal chart.

Lord. A sign-ruler.

Lord (of a Planet). The planet that rules the sign containing the planet under consideration.

Lords of the Triplicity. A set of three planets that rules a triplicity (q.v.). They are numbered: First Lord, Second Lord, and Third Lord.

Lord of Time. *See* Light of Time.

Lords of the Anauba. Same as Lords of the Triplicity. *See* Chapt. 7, note 30.

Lot. An older term for Part (q.v.).

Luminaries. *See* Lights.

Made fortunate. The opposite of impedited (q.v.). A planet is made fortunate by being well placed in the zodiac and in the circle of houses and by receiving a good aspect, especially from a Benefic (q.v.).

Malefic. A planet that is naturally evil by nature: Mars and Saturn.

Masculine Quarter. The quadrant from the ASC to the MC and the one opposite it are masculine.

Masculine Sign. One of the odd-numbered signs: Aries, Gemini, etc.

MC. The *Medium Caeli* or Midheaven (q.v.).

MC Degree. The midheaven degree or cusp of the 10th house. In the Equal House system, it is always 90° behind the ASC Degree in the zodiac. But in the later, quadrantal systems, it is the degree of the zodiac that intersects the prime meridian above the earth, and is thus the *astronomical* midheaven.

Midheaven. The 10th house of a chart. The term is sometimes used to refer to the MC Degree.

Mobile Sign. One of the four signs, Aries, Cancer, Libra, or Capricorn. Now usually called "cardinal signs."

Moist Signs. The air and water signs: Gemini, Cancer, Libra, Scorpio, Aquarius, and Pisces.

Nativity. A natal chart or horoscope (qq.v.) It is an inceptional figure, and as such can be drawn for the "birth" of anything (e.g., the launching of a ship, or opening the doors of a business for the first time). But the term *nativity* is restricted to creatures that are born, and especially to humans. It is obsolescent in modern astrology, the terms *horoscope* and *(birth)chart* being preferred.

New Moon Nativity. A natal horoscope for which the preceding lunation was a new Moon.

Nocturnal Nativity. A natal horoscope with the Sun below the horizon.

Nocturnal Planet. One of the planets that is said to "rejoice" by night, viz. the Moon, Venus, and Mars. Mercury is nocturnal when it sets after the Sun.

Node. One of the two points where the orbital plane of the Moon or a planet intersects the ecliptic circle. The node where the moving body crosses from south to north is called the *ascending* node and the one where it crosses from north to south is called the *descending* node. The ancients referred to these as the Dragon's Head and the Dragon's Tail (qq.v.) or simply the Head and the Tail.

Occidental. The 2nd and 4th quadrants from the Sun or from the ASC degree in the clockwise direction.

Occidental Planet. A planet in an occidental quadrant. (If the quadrantal reference is to the Sun, it is usually so stated.)

Opposition. A configuration in which two points are either exactly
    180° apart in the zodiac or within a few degrees of being 180°
    apart. The points can be planets, house cusps, parts, fixed
    stars, etc. The word is also used to refer to the opposition of
    the Sun and Moon (i.e., the Full Moon), especially in the
    phrase "the preceding opposition," which refers to the full
    Moon that preceded the moment for which a chart is drawn. (See
    Full Moon Nativity.)

Orb. The distance on either side of a planet through which its
    influence extends. (Sometimes used in the plural with no
    difference in meaning.) Abu 'Ali does not specify a precise
    value, but figures in the range of 8° - 12° are typical. The
    lights and Jupiter usually have the largest values, while
    Mercury has the smallest.

Oriental. The 1st and 3rd quadrants from the Sun or from the ASC
    degree in the clockwise direction.

Oriental Planet. A planet in an oriental quadrant. (If the quadrantal
    reference is to the Sun, it is usually so stated.)

Part. A sensitive point in the zodiac determined by calculating the
    distance between one point and another point and adding the
    distance to a third point. Most commonly, the first and second
    points are planets and the third point is the ASC degree. In
    classical astrology, they were called *lots* because they were
    used to determine the prospects for a particular thing. In
    modern astrology, they are usually called the *Arabic Parts*
    because only the Part of Fortune (q.v.) is mentioned by
    Ptolemy, and all the other parts are mistakenly assumed to have
    been invented by the Arabs.

Partile. Said of an aspect (q.v.) when it is exact to within 1°,
    especially when the degrees have the same number, e.g. Sun in
    12 Aries partile square Mars in 12 Cancer. It is considered to
    be more powerful than an aspect that is only *platic* (q.v.),
    i.e. within orbs but not partile.

Part of Fortune. The most famous of the parts. Calculated by day from
    the Sun to the Moon and cast from the ASC degree; but by night,
    from the Moon to the Sun and cast from the ASC degree. (Ptolemy
    used the day formula for both day and night, but the ancient
    and medieval astrologers generally used the original two-
    formula method. However, the Ptolemaic simplification has
    become standard among modern astrologers.)

Peregrine. Said of a planet when it is in a degree of the zodiac
    where it is in none of its five dignities (q.v.).

Place. The classical term for one of the 12 divisions of the
    horoscope chart. Medieval writers more often use the term
    "house," but sometimes use the older term "place." Thus, the
    expression "badly placed" usually means "in a bad house."

Planet. A celestial body that moves through the zodiac. Thus, it
    includes the Sun and the Moon as well as the planets.

Platic. An aspect that is within orbs (q.v.) but not exact or partile
    (q.v.). It is considered to be weaker than a partile aspect.

Profection. A symbolic progression in a chart used for
    prognostication.

Profection of the Year. A symbolic progression that begins at the ASC
    degree and moves forward in the zodiac at the rate of 30° per
    year. See Chapt. 1, note 10. An ancient predictive method that
    has been virtually abandoned by modern astrologers.

Progression. The motion of a planet or house cusp immediately
    following the moment for which a chart is drawn. A primary
    progression is motion due to the rotation of the earth. For
    example, if the Sun is on the ASC degree at birth, then by
    primary progression it rises towards the MC (or it can be
    considered to remain "fixed" and to be successively aspected by
    the other planets as they rotate). Likewise, the ASC degree
    moves forward through the zodiac. Such motion is equated to
    years of the native's life at the rate of 4 minutes of time to
    1 year.

Prorogative Places. The houses in a natal horoscope where a planet
    must be to be eligible to be designated as Prorogator (q.v.).
    See Chapt. 2.

Prorogator. A term used to translate the Greek word aphetes used by
    Ptolemy (Tetrabiblos, iii. 10) to designate the Significator of
    Life in a natal horoscope. The Arabic term Hyleg (q.v.) has
    largely replaced it in astrological literature.

Ray. Older term for Aspect (q.v.).

Retrograde. Said of a planet when it is moving backward in the
    zodiac.

Revolution of Years. A method of judging future prospects by erecting
    a chart for the moment when the Sun returns to the degree and
    minute it occupied at the native's birth. The revolutionary
    figure is compared to the natal horoscope according to a
    special set of rules. It gives indications of the native's life
    from the birthday for which it is set until the next one.
    Modern astrologers call the revolutionary figure a "solar
    return."

Rising Sign. The sign of the zodiac that is on the eastern horizon at
    a given moment. Sometimes called the "ascending sign." In the
    Sign-House system of celestial houses, it constitutes the 1st
    house or ASC. In the later systems, it is the sign in which the
    ASC degree is placed.

Royal Signs. The signs of the Fire Triplicity: Aries, Leo, and
    Sagittarius.

Second Lord of the Triplicity. *See* Triplicity.

Separation. An aspect between two planets that has already passed
     exactitude, but is still within orbs (q.v.).

Sign. One of the twelfth parts of the zodiac measured from the
     beginning of Aries. The early astrologers who used the Sign-
     House and Equal House systems of house division, often used the
     word "sign" instead of "house." Thus, the phrase "Mars in the
     6th sign" means "Mars in the 6th house."

Sign-House. A modern name for the oldest system of house division, in
     which the rising sign constituted the 1st house, the next sign
     the 2nd house, etc. This was the primitive form of the so-
     called Equal House system (q.v.).

Sign of the Full Moon. The sign in which the Moon is placed at the
     moment when it is exactly opposite the Sun.

Sign of the New Moon. The sign in which the Moon is placed at the
     moment when it is exactly conjoined to the Sun.

Significator. A planet that signifies or rules a matter under
     consideration. It is selected according to specific rules.

Signs of few children. Leo, Virgo, Capricorn, and Aquarius. (*See*
     Chapt. 12.)

Signs of many children. Cancer, Scorpio, and Pisces. (*See* Chapt. 12.)

Star. A planet or a fixed star. In the ancient and medieval writers,
     the term used by itself usually means a planet rather than a
     fixed star. (Note that the word "planet" can refer to the Sun
     or the Moon in classical and medieval astrology.) Modern
     English-speaking astrologers sometimes use the word in this
     sense if they are speaking familiarly or poetically, but they
     customarily speak of *planets* and *fixed stars*.

Succedent House. The 2nd, 5th, 8th, and 11th houses are succedent.

Tail. *See* Dragon's Tail.

Terms. Properly, the *limits* of the five areas within each sign ruled
     by one of the planets. The word is used in either the plural or
     the singular to denote one of the areas, as "Mars in the
     term(s) of Saturn." There are several systems of terms. Since
     Abu 'Ali's book is in the Dorothean tradition, he presumably
     used the *Egyptian* terms.

Testimony. Used figuratively to refer to the individual circumstances
     of a planet in the chart under consideration. Thus, Mercury
     might have three testimonies, consisting of being angular, in
     its own sign, and receiving a sextile from Jupiter; at the same
     time, Mercury "gives testimony" to Jupiter by virtue of its
     aspect to it.

Third Lord of the Triplicity. *See* Triplicity.

Triplicity. A group of three signs at 120° intervals, e.g. Aries,
Leo, and Sagittarius. Each of these groups is assigned to an
element (the one just mentioned to Fire). Ancient tradition
that goes back at least to Dorotheus (1st century A.D.)
assigned a set of three planets as "lords" of each triplicity
(Sun, Jupiter, and Saturn for the Fire triplicity). The first
one mentioned is the "first lord," the second, the "second
lord," and the third, the "third lord." By night, the first two
reverse, and the (day) first lord becomes the (night) second
lord, and vice versa. The third stays put. Dorotheus assigns
them to the beginning, the middle, and the end of time periods.

Under the Sunbeams. Said of a planet when it is more than 8°30' but
less than 17° from the Sun.

Years (of a Planet). A characteristic number of years that is
assigned to a planet according to its strength. For each planet
there are three numbers: Greater, Medium, and Lesser (sometimes
called Major, Middling, and Minor). See the table in Chapt. 4.
(The greater numbers are the sums of the Egyptian terms. The
lesser numbers are related to the periods of the planets. The
Medium numbers are the means of the greater and lesser
numbers.) In certain cases, the same numbers are used to
indicate months, days, or even hours.

Zodiac. The ecliptic circle subdivided into 12 signs. Since Ptolemy's
tables came into use, the zodiac begins at the vernal equinox
(an innovation that goes back to Hipparchus in the 2nd century
B.C.). The change-over took place in the 3rd or 4th century, at
which time there was about 3° difference between the older
Hellenistic "fixed" zodiac and the new "tropical" zodiac. By
the end of the 5th century, the difference had dropped to zero,
and they were both about about 2.5° from the actual tropical
zodiac.

                              NOTE.

    Some of the terms above do not occur in the translation but are
added for the reader's convenience. References to chapters refer to
Abu 'Ali's book unless otherwise stated.

BIBLIOGRAPHY

Abu 'Ali al-Khayyat
  Albohali Arabis astrologi antiquissimi
  ac clarissimi de iudiciis Natiuitatum.
  [Albohali, a most Ancient and Famous Arabian
  Astrologer, On the Judgments of Nativities.]
  Ed. by Joachim Heller.
  Nûrnberg: Montani & Neuber, 1546.

Abu Ma'shar
  Introductorius maior.
  [Greater Introduction.]
  Trans. by John of Seville
  (never printed, cited from MS)

Al-Biruni, Abu'l-Rayḥan
  The Book of Instruction in the Elements
  of the Art of Astrology.
  Trans. by R. Ramsay Wright.
  London: Luzac & Co., 1934.

Al-Nadim, Muḥammad ibn Isḥaq
  The Fihrist of al-Nadim.
  Ed. & trans. by Bayard Dodge
  New York: Columbia Univ. Press, 1970.

Bonatti, Guido
  Decem tractatus astronomie.
  [Ten Treatises of Astrology.]
  Augsburg: Erhard Ratdolt, 1491.

Carmody, Francis J
  Arabic Astronomical and Astrological
  Sciences in Latin Translation.
  Berkeley and Los Angeles: Univ. of Calif. Press, 1956.

CCAG (abbrev. for the series following)
    Catalogus Codicum Astrologorum Graecorum. 12 vols.
    [Catalogue of Greek Astrological Manuscripts.]
    Brussels: Belgian Royal Academy, 1898-1953.

Dorotheus Sidonius
    Carmen astrologicum.
    Ed. & trans. by David Pingree.
    Leipzig: B.G. Teubner, 1976.

Firmicus Maternus, Julius
    Matheseos libri viii.
    Trans. by Jean Rhys Bram, as
    Ancient Astrology Theory and Practice.
    Park Ridge, N.J.: Noyes Press, 1975.

Heliodorus
    In Paulum Alexandrinum commentarium.
    [Commentary on Paul of Alexandria.]
    ed. by E. Boer.
    Leipzig: B.G. Teubner, 1962.

Ibn Ezra, Abraham ben Meir
    The Beginning of Wisdom.
    Ed. & trans. by Raphael Levy and Francisco Cantera.
    Baltimore: Johns Hopkins Press, 1939.

John of Seville
    Epitome astrologiae.
    [Epitome of Astrology.]
    Ed. by Joachim Heller.
    Nürnberg: Montani & Neuber, 1548.

Kennedy, E.S. and Pingree, David
    The Astrological History of Masha'allah.
    Cambridge, Mass.: Harvard Univ. Press, 1971.

Leopold of Austria
    *Compilatio Leupoldi ducatus Austrie
    filii de astrorum scientia.*
    [Compilation on the Science of the Stars.]
    Augsburg: Erhard Ratdolt, 1489.

Lilly, William
Christian Astrology.
London: Partridge & Blunden, 1647. 1st ed.
Exeter: Regulus Publ. Co., 1985. 3rd ed. (facs. repr. of 1647)

Morin, Jean Baptiste
    Astrologia Gallica.
    [French Astrology.]
    The Hague, 1661.

    *The Morinus System of Horoscope Interpretation/
    Astrologia Gallica Book Twenty One.*
    Trans. by Richard S. Baldwin
    Washington: Am. Fed. of Astrologers, 1974.

Neugebauer, O. and Van Hoesen, H.B.
    Greek Horoscopes.
    Memoirs of the Am. Philos. Society. vol. 48.
    Philadelphia: American Phil. Society, 1959.

Newton, Robert R.
    The Crime of Claudius Ptolemy.
    Baltimore: Johns Hopkins Univ. Press, 1977.

Paul of Alexandria
    Elementa apotelesmatica.
    [Introduction to Astrology]
    ed. by E. Boer.
    Leipzig: B.G. Teubner, 1958.

Ptolemy, Claudius
    Tetrabiblos.
    Ed. & trans. by F.E. Robbins
    Loeb Classical Library.
    Cambridge, Mass.: Harvard Univ. Press, 1940.

Wilson, James
    (A Complete) Dictionary of Astrology.
    London: W. Hughes, 1819. 1st ed.
    Boston: A.H. Roffe & Co., 1885. repr. ed.
    New York: Samuel Weiser, 1969. facs. repr. of 1885 ed.